countering fraud for competitive advantage

the professional approach to reducing the last great hidden cost

Mark Button & Jim Gee

WILEY

A John Wiley & Sons, Ltd., Publication

Registered office
John Wiley & Sons Ltd, The Atrium, Southern Gate, Chichester, West Sussex, PO19 8SQ, United Kingdom

For details of our global editorial offices, for customer services and for information about how to apply for permission to reuse the copyright material in this book please see our website at www.wiley.com.

Library of Congress Cataloging-in-Publication Data

Button, Mark, 1969–
Countering fraud for competitive advantage : the professional approach to reducing the last great hidden cost / Mark Button and Jim Gee.
pages cm
Includes bibliographical references and index.
ISBN 978-1-119-99474-9 (hardback)
1. Fraud–Prevention. 2. Employee theft–Prevention. 3. Auditing, Internal. I. Gee, Jim, 1957– II. Title.
HV6691.G44 2013
658.4′73–dc23

2012045977

A catalogue record for this book is available from the British Library.

ISBN 978-1-119-99474-9 (hardback) ISBN 978-1-118-45425-1 (ebk)
ISBN 978-1-119-96040-9 (ebk) ISBN 978-1-119-96041-6 (ebk)

Set in 11/13pt Times by Aptara Inc., New Delhi, India
Printed in Great Britain by TJ International Ltd, Padstow, Cornwall, UK

Contents

1
Introduction

In an era of tighter budgets and more competitive markets, organisations are looking for innovative ways to reduce costs and increase profits. Many strategies and innovative ideas have been pursued and advocated by gurus, from contracting out to flatter management structures. Much is made of their potential to achieve what is often described as 'competitive advantage'.[1] Business schools in universities around the world are full of academics who advocate lots of ways to achieve this. One measure, however, has not been on the 'radar' of the vast majority – investing in measures to counter fraud. This is largely because fraud is a hidden cost. Frequently it is not measured, or it is gauged using detected fraud losses, which hide the true costs. This book will show that it is reasonable to assume that in most organisations fraud losses are around 5 per cent, something ACFE, through less valid research, have been showing for some time.[2] Now consider 5 per cent of the procurement budget or payroll in your organisation; in most cases that would amount to a significant sum of money. The good news is that there are measures to substantially reduce this, and the application of appropriate methods can reap 30 per cent plus reductions in fraud losses. This can be done relatively cheaply, thus producing returns on investment of 12 × or more.[3] This book will outline a model to achieve this: the professional approach to reducing fraud – the last great hidden cost – to reap competitive advantage.

There are lots of books on the market which tell you how to prevent or investigate fraud. Some of these are very good. However, they all miss one obvious point – fraud is a business cost like staff, capital, marketing etc. All organisations suffer from fraud, even if they think they don't because there have been no detected frauds. Most frauds by their nature are undetected, and fraud costs money. Because of the lack of accurate measurement, it is the last great cost many organisations unknowingly have, which could also be substantially reduced. In the commercial sector this could reap a competitive advantage, and in the increasingly financially strained public sector, it could stave off cuts in services. *Countering Fraud for Competitive Advantage* (*CFCA*) therefore offers more than a book on how to prevent and investigate fraud. It offers a completely new way of looking at the problem and a holistic model for countering it.

There are some organisations which don't even compile regular statistics on detected frauds, because they are seen as unusual and rare. Others do use statistics, but focus on detected frauds. Such measures are flawed because many frauds are undetected and many go on for a long time before they are detected. Our research shows that average losses from fraud and error are around 5 per cent. In many organisations this is even higher. So consider an organisation with a $100 million turnover: if they are performing in an average way they could be losing around $5 million to fraud. Now just answer the four questions below about what you are currently doing to counter fraud:

- Do you *accurately* measure fraud losses?
- Do you have an independent hotline which is well publicised to report fraud and abuse?
- Do you pursue measures to develop an anti-fraud culture?
- Do you use data-mining and matching to conduct pro-active investigations?

If the answer to any of these is no you are at higher risk of fraud and you are likely to be above average in fraud losses, so the $100 million organisation could be losing well over $5 million to fraud. Similarly consider the traits of an organisation at higher risk from fraud from its staff:

- Staff with perception that they are poorly paid;
- Staff with perception that they have poor conditions of employment;
- Staff with high levels of job dissatisfaction;
- Large number of staff wanting to leave;
- Tolerance of petty crime/fraud; and
- Immoral/unethical working practices.

If any of these apply to your organisation you may be at greater risk of fraud. Also consider one of the most common reasons perfectly law-abiding and honest employees turn to fraud: personal financial problems. The USA, UK and many other countries are in the midst of one of the worst recessions since the end of the Second World War. This has led to many people losing their jobs, downgrading to lower-paid work, having to take pay cuts, losing over-time, living in houses with negative equity so they are unable to move, amongst many others. Indeed in America an article on the impact of the recession found that:

- More than half the adult workforce has experienced a 'work-related hardship' of unemployment, a pay cut, reduction in working hours or an involuntary move to part-time employment;
- Over 70 per cent of Americans over the age of 40 have been affected by the economic crisis;
- The net worth of the average American household has shrunk by 20 per cent;
- Long-term unemployment is at the highest levels since the 1940s; and
- 20 per cent of Americans have seen a 25 per cent or greater reduction in household income.[4]

Consider some of the impacts on the UK which have been noted:

- Around 1.2 million local government workers have experienced a pay freeze for three years, which amounts to a 15 per cent pay reduction in real terms;[5]
- From 2011, UK public sector workers were told to expect pay rises of no more than 1 per cent for two years with 710,000 workers to lose their jobs by 2017;[6]
- Since the recession began, unemployment in the UK has risen from 1.61 million in December 2007 to 2.67 million in December 2011 – an increase of over 1 million;[7]
- All this has occurred at a time when inflation has regularly been between 3 and 5 per cent; and[8]
- A study for the Yorkshire and Clydesdale Banks has also claimed that 2 million families feel under strain due to financial and money worries.[9]

Consider how many of your staff and families might be experiencing some of the above. Most will not turn to fraud as a consequence, but some will.

CFCA, however, will set out a holistic strategy to counter fraud which has been shown to produce a 12 to 1 return on investment.[10] Fraud losses can be reduced at a very reasonable cost and those saved resources can be used to enhance profitability in the commercial sector, or be invested in frontline services in the public and not-for-profit sectors.

This book is aimed at those who run organisations and want them to be more financially healthy and stable. It is aimed at those who directly undertake counter-fraud work and who want to be more effective and see greater tangible results. And it is aimed at all those who suffer from the cost of fraud currently being too high – shareholders whose companies are not as profitable as they might be; employees whose job security is undermined; taxpayers who do not get the quality of public services that they pay for; and those donating to charities where the charitable purpose is undermined. We all have a stake in fraud being tackled effectively.

1.1 BOOK OUTLINE

In the next chapter we begin by considering what fraud is; the diversity of it as well as the scale of it. It will show how diverse it can be as well as how significant a drain it can represent on an organisation. The chapter will also consider what the impact of fraud on an organisation can be.

In Chapter 3 the book considers the fraudster and the culture of fraud. There has been limited interest in fraud amongst researchers, but the chapter unpicks some of the research to reveal types, profiles and the motivation of fraudsters. Culture also plays a very important part in influencing levels of fraud and this chapter examines some of the factors contributing to this.

The resilience of organisations and countries to fraud is the subject of Chapter 4. The chapter shows that resources and attention on fraud at a national level is often lacking. This is also often replicated in the strategies to counter fraud. Data on the quality of organisations' strategies to counter fraud are explored.

In Chapter 5 the book turns to strategies which can be used to reduce fraud. This chapter focuses upon the mechanics of measuring fraud and how this is very important in the overall strategy to counter fraud. The chapter describes the basic principles of fraud measurement and examines how this should shape the overall counter-fraud strategy.

Changing attitudes towards fraud is as important as measures to prevent fraud. There are a very wide range of measures which can be used to achieve these aims. Chapter 6 builds upon the research on fraudsters, as well as the extensive crime prevention research to demonstrate a wide range of tools to prevent fraud and create an anti-fraud culture.

Unfortunately it is never possible to prevent all frauds and those that do occur need to be detected quickly, and investigated to the highest standards. In Chapter 7 the tools to detect and investigate fraud effectively are examined. In doing so the chapter draws upon some of the extensive research from psychology for detecting deception.

Once an investigation has been completed there is a wide range of options open to an organisation to sanction the fraudster and secure redress. Chapter 8 will show that the traditional criminal sanctions are only one of many that a fully equipped counter-fraud professional can use.

Central to this book is making fraud a cost. In Chapter 9 the importance of this metric, as well as many others, is identified. The chapter examines the importance of metrics (or key performance indicators as some call them) and how they can be created for an organisation. Some of the potential drawbacks are also explored.

Much of what is advocated in this book could not be undertaken without professional counter-fraud staff who possess the appropriate knowledge and skills. They are needed to influence the organisation towards this professional approach, to develop the strategy, to lead on developing an anti-fraud culture and prevention, to detect and investigate fraud, to pursue sanctions and redress, and to manage performance. Chapter 10 explores the origin of these functions, what they need to do and why organisations should invest in them.

In the final chapter the model is drawn together and reasonable reductions in fraud losses are applied to the leading companies in the world, the USA, UK, France and Germany. The chapter shows the substantial gains in profitability some companies could achieve if they pursued the professional approach to countering fraud.

END NOTES

1. See for example Porter, M.E. (2004) *Competitive Advantage*. New York: Free Press; Briggs, R. and Edwards, C. (2006) *The Business of Resilience*. London: Demos; Champy, J. and Hammer, M. (1993) *Reengineering the Corporation: a Manifesto for Business Revolution*. New York: Harper Collins; Hamel, G. and Prahalad, C.K. (1996) *Competing for the Future*. Harvard: Harvard Business School Press. See also http://www.time.com/time/specials/packages/completelist/0,29569,2086680,00 .html for the 25 most influential business books.
2. See ACFE (2010) *Report to the Nation on Occupational Fraud and Abuse*. Austin: ACFE; and Gee, J. Button, M. and Brooks, G. (2011) *The Financial Cost of Fraud. What the data from around the world shows*. London: PKF/CCFS.
3. NHSCFSMS (2007) *Countering Fraud in the NHS: Protecting Resources for Patients. 1999–2006 Performance Statistics*. London: CFSMS.
4. Warner, J. (2010) What the Great Recession Has Done to Family Life. *New York Times*. http://www.nytimes.com/2010/08/08/magazine/08FOB-wwln-t.html.
5. New Policy Institute (2012) Living on the Edge: Pay in Local Government. Retrieved 12 April 2012 from http://www.unison.org.uk/acrobat/5821.pdf.

6. BBC News (2011) Osborne Confirms Pay and Jobs Pain as Growth Slows. Retrieved 12 April 2012 from http://www.bbc.co.uk/news/uk-politics-15931086.
7. BBC News (2012) Business Tracker. Retrieved 12 April 2012 from http://www.bbc.co.uk/news/10604117.
8. BBC News (2012) Economy Tracker. Retrieved 12 April 2012 from http://www.bbc.co.uk/news/10612209.
9. Top News (2010) Impact of the Recession in the Lives of Families. Retrieved 12 April 2012 from http://topnews.us/content/221202-impact-recession-lives-families.
10. NHSCFSMS (2007) op. cit.

2

The Fraud Problem

2.1 INTRODUCTION

In most organisations the fraud problem is under-estimated because senior managers confuse detected levels of fraud with the real level of fraud, and detected levels are often very low or even zero. This chapter will seek to dispel this myth. It will begin by illustrating the fraud iceberg which shows the detected levels of fraud as the small tip above the surface, but with the substantial undetected frauds below the surface. The chapter will then shock the reader with the wide variety of ways fraud can occur in an organisation. The amount of fraud an organisation can expect to suffer from will then be examined. It will show a loss rate of around 5 per cent to be normal, with much higher rates also possible. A brief analysis of recent trends in fraud will be undertaken to highlight the increasing risk. Finally the chapter will consider the impact of fraud and show that the effect upon an organisation is more than financial.

2.2 THE FRAUD PROBLEM

A very common view amongst many senior employees in organisations is that 'there is no fraud in my patch'. This view is largely driven by the line of thought that if there is no detected fraud, then there can't be any fraud. When the authors discuss their and others' research with senior managers, which suggests levels of fraud around 5 per cent as average, they often just look bemused and cannot comprehend that their organisation could suffer such losses from fraud.

What these and many managers are doing is mistaking detected fraud for the true measure of fraud. Detected fraud, however, is the tip of the iceberg. Many frauds are never detected and many go undetected for a long time (some forever). Indeed the Association of Certified Fraud Examiners (ACFE) estimates that the median length of time internal frauds last before being detected is 18 months.[1] Some actions are also disputed as to whether they are fraud, but may well come close to it. By its very nature most fraud is invisible with the malefactor determined to hide all

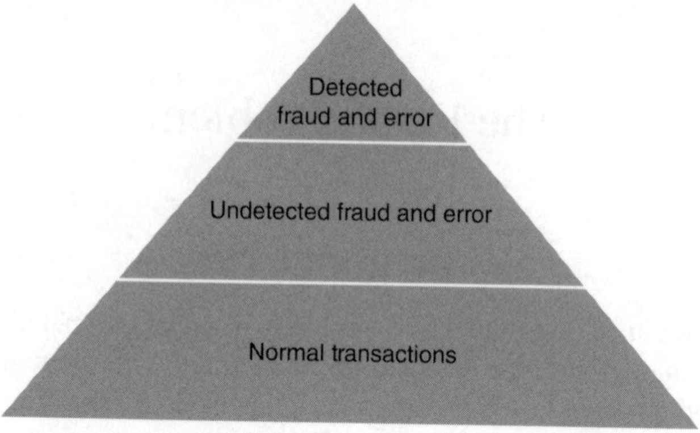

Figure 2.1 The Fraud and Error Pyramid

traces of it. Thus what will be the real situation in most organisations is a tiny number of detected frauds and a substantially larger number of undetected frauds, as the pyramid in Figure 2.1 illustrates.

2.2.1 What is Fraud?

Fraud encompasses a wide range of behaviours. What unites most definitions is the act of deception to perpetrate the crime; as Wells argues, fraud is 'any crime which uses deception as its principal modus operandi'.[2] Legally there is also the distinction between civil and criminal definitions. The starting point for civil law definitions of fraud in England and Wales is the case of *Derry v Peek* (1889) (UK House of Lords). Here, Lord Herschell, giving judgement on the case, defined 'fraud' to include a false statement 'made knowingly, or without belief in its truth, or recklessly, careless whether it be true or false'. This definition covers a number of possibilities, ranging from:

- where a person admits knowledge that a statement is untrue; through to . . .
- where it can be demonstrated from evidence that they knew the statement to be untrue (even if this is not admitted); through to . . .
- where it can be demonstrated from evidence that they did not care whether the statement was true or untrue – or in other words, that they knew it was possible that the statement might be untrue.

In 2005 the Swiss Institute of Comparative Law provided the following definition, which broadly follows the English law:

> Civil fraud is the use or presentation of false, incorrect or incomplete statements and/or documents, or the non-disclosure of information in violation of a legally enforceable obligation to disclose, having as its effect the misappropriation or wrongful retention of funds or property of others, or their misuse for purposes other than those specified.[3]

In England and Wales the criminal definition of fraud has been codified with the passage of the Fraud Act 2006.[4] There are a huge number of advantages this new law brings and there is much to debate about the use of it. As this book is aimed at an international audience, only the main provisions of it will be outlined. Those interested in it further should review Farrell et al.'s book.[5] This sets out a number of ways in which fraud can be committed:

- Fraud by False Representation (this could cover the submission of false over-time sheets or a false invoice for services by a person).
- Fraud by Failing to Disclose Information (this could be a where a person is paid for 40 hours per week, but in fact only works 30 and fails to disclose this, or a prospective employee is asked for certain information on the application form but doesn't provide it).
- Fraud by Abuse of Position (this is where a person in a position of trust abuses their position, such as an accountant diverting funds to their own personal account).

The legislation also set out a series of other offences such as:

- Possession of articles for use in frauds and making or supplying articles for use in frauds (this is very wide ranging and could include catching someone at home with a paper or electronic copy of a false invoice which could be submitted to a company).
- Participating in a fraudulent business (this could be a car dealership founded on enhancing the value of cars by turning back the mileage clocks).
- Obtaining services dishonestly (this could be securing an insurance policy by providing false or inaccurate information).

In addition to this the old common law offence of conspiracy to defraud was maintained, which gives wide scope to the potential behaviours when two or more are acting together. Various fraud-related offences in sectors/activities were also maintained in social security, elections, forgery and counterfeiting, false accounting, insider dealing, etc.

It is also common to link fraud with corruption. Corruption is also very broad, covering a wide range of behaviours. The Asian Development Bank defines corruption as:

> ... behaviour on the part of officials in the public and private sectors, in which they improperly and unlawfully enrich themselves and/or those close to them, or induce others to do so, by misusing the position in which they are placed.[6]

Central to corruption is bribery, where a person covertly pays someone in a position of power to act in a particular way, where such payments are not allowed. Clearly there are elements of fraud where a person in a position of responsibility abuses that position by accepting a bribe. Thus many examples of occupational fraud where an employee is involved can also be seen as corruption. But the person paying the bribe may not be committing a fraud. There are also many frauds committed which do not involve the abuse of a position of responsibility, such as an external person submitting false invoices to a company to be paid. It is important to note that this book is focused upon fraud, but that clearly because of the overlap (see Figure 2.2) corruption is considered as well. It is not the intention, however, to become deeply involved in the different aspects of corruption.

It would now seem appropriate after this brief legal description of fraud to consider the huge variety of fraud, by illustrating some of the many diverse types.

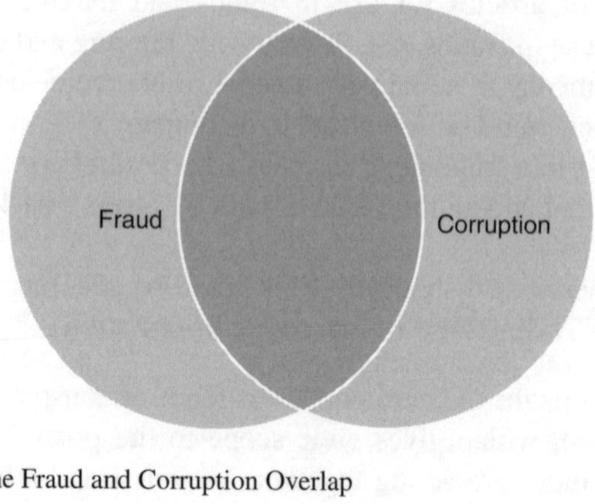

Figure 2.2 The Fraud and Corruption Overlap

2.2.2 Types of Fraud

Senior managers in organisations therefore need to be aware that there are numerous ways employees, contractors, suppliers, clients, etc. can defraud their organisation if they do not have an appropriate counter-fraud strategy in place. Fraudsters are often very creative and there is a risk in virtually every aspect of a business. To illustrate this we will now identify 43 ways that fraud can occur in an organisation. This list is by no means exhaustive.

1. Accounting fraud. Employee moves monies into personal bank account.
2. Accounting fraud. Employee changes payee to their name or company from the legitimate payee.
3. Accounting fraud. Employee 'washes' cheques to change name of payee to themselves or their company.
4. Employee fraud. Employee uses personal banking data from clients, such as credit card numbers, for fraudulent purchases.
5. Employee fraud. A corrupt employee sells or uses personal information of clients for the purpose of committing identity fraud.
6. Employee fraud. Employee writes off equipment as obsolete/damaged when it is not, and then acquires it.
7. Employee fraud. Employee uses organisation's resources for private interests without approval.
8. Employee fraud. Employee conducts private work in breach of contract without proper approval.
9. Employee fraud. Employee goes off sick, claims sick pay when not sick.
10. Employee fraud. Employee goes off sick, claims sick pay and then works for another organisation or in another capacity.
11. Employee fraud. Employee has outside interests which are not declared when taking decisions related to them.
12. Employment fraud. Prospective employee submits false qualifications to secure job.
13. Employment fraud. Prospective employee submits false documents regarding their immigration status to secure job.
14. Employment fraud. Prospective employee lies about their past experience to secure job.
15. Employment fraud. Prospective employee sets up false referees to secure job.

16. Employment fraud. Employer turns blind eye to immigration status of employees.
17. Employment fraud. Employer turns blind eye to employee claiming social security benefits.
18. Employment fraud. Employer pays staff cash-in-hand to avoid having to pay tax, etc.
19. Employment fraud. Prospective employee impersonates another person to secure a job.
20. Expenses fraud. Employee submits fictional expenses.
21. Expenses fraud. Employee submits claim for expenses above what was actual expense.
22. Expenses fraud. Employee claims for first/business class travel and then cashes it in buying a lower class ticket and pocketing the difference.
23. Expenses fraud. An employee with a company credit card uses it for personal purchases but claims they are for the business.
24. Expenses fraud. Employee changes details of what expenditure was really for, such as replacing lap-dancing club with restaurant.
25. Expenses fraud. Employee submits same expense claim more than once.
26. Identity fraud. A fraudster uses counterfeit website/documents, etc. to trick clients into parting with sensitive personal information, or paying them instead of the real body.
27. Investment fraud. Company engages in conduct to unlawfully boost its real financial situation in order to boost share price.
28. Investment fraud. Staff use inside information to make advantageous stock purchases/sales.
29. Litigation fraud. A customer or employee submits a legal claim for damages which is fictitious.
30. Litigation fraud. A customer or employee submits an exaggerated claim for damages.
31. Payroll fraud. 'Ghost employees' are added to the payroll with salary paid to fraudsters' and/or associates' accounts.
32. Payroll fraud. Additional salary increments are added without proper approval to fraudster and/or associates.
33. Payroll fraud. Additional overtime is added to the fraudster's pay which has not been undertaken or authorized.
34. Payroll fraud. Additional allowances are added to pay without approval.

35. Procurement fraud. Supplier offers bribe to purchaser to favour their bid.
36. Procurement fraud. Supplier offers bribe to purchaser to give inside information.
37. Procurement fraud. Supplier submits invoice for services/goods not provided.
38. Procurement fraud. Suppler submits invoices for goods/services more than once.
39. Procurement fraud. Supplier submits invoice for counterfeit/substandard goods or services.
40. Procurement fraud. Employee orders goods and services from supplier with no intention of paying for them.
41. Procurement fraud. Employee sets up company which submits invoices for non-existent services/products.
42. Procurement fraud. Employee or external person uses forged documentation to write to company detailing change of account for invoices to be paid to from the legitimate one to their own.
43. Procurement fraud. Employee orders extra goods which their employer pays for but which they use for themselves or sell on to make a profit.

It is important to note that the list above is not exhaustive. Fraud is a dynamic crime which is constantly changing with fraudsters identifying new ways to perpetrate it. Now if we return to the sceptical senior manager in an organisation and ask the question: does their organisation suffer from fraud? Can they really go through the above list of frauds and – just because none have been detected – honestly say that none of these are occurring? The reality is that in most organisations it will vary according to a variety of factors which will gradually be unfolded in this book. But almost all will have a good number of these frauds occurring. Every year PKF produces a list of the 10 worst frauds. Below in the box are the bottom five from 2011 – which also illustrates the diversity of the risk of fraud. The next section will draw upon research to illustrate how much fraud an organisation can expect to have.

Bottom Five Frauds of 2011[7]

5. PET INSURANCE FRAUD ON THE RISE

A woman was jailed for nine months after fraudulently claiming £37,000 to cover the cost of treating her non-existent pet dogs. The woman created fake vets' bills in order to receive payment from her insurance company. Worryingly, there has been a growing number of reports of owners selling, abandoning or even killing pets in order to claim for early death.

4. MILLIONS MISUSED IN RAILWAY PROJECT

The Chinese National Audit Office (NAO) revealed that 187 million Yuan (around £20 million) was misappropriated by individuals or companies involved in building the 1,318-km Beijing–Shanghai high-speed railway. The announcement followed the dismissal of railways minister Liu Zhijun.

3. GANG USED BLEACH TO MAKE ILLICIT VODKA

A UK man was jailed for seven years for manufacturing thousands of bottles of fake vodka using methylated spirits and bleach. Investigators estimated that 165,000 bottles of the falsely-branded Glen's Vodka had been made before the fraudster and his team were apprehended.

2. TAX EVADERS JAILED AFTER CARBON PERMIT TRADING SCAM

Six men were jailed in Germany for a 300 million Euro (around £249 million) fraud involving carbon emission permits. Three Britons, two Germans and a Frenchman bought the permits overseas without paying any tax, then resold the permits to each other in order to fraudulently claim the tax back. The judge told the perpetrators that they had brought 'the carbon market trading scheme into disrepute.'

1. FAKE CANCER DRUGS GIVEN TO THOUSANDS

A chartered accountant from Windsor was jailed for eight years for importing fake drugs from China and selling them as genuine medicines for cancer, heart conditions and mental illness. The medicines were used by pharmacies, hospitals and care homes, and it is believed that at least 100,000 doses ended up being given to patients. The accountant was caught after a wholesaler spotted a mistake on the packaging.

2.3 THE EXTENT OF FRAUD

The discussion of fraud above sheds some light on the challenges of measuring fraud. This section will now illustrate, using a variety of measures, the likely scale of the problem of fraud in an organisation. Broadly there are two types of indicators of fraud: those that identify the number of frauds and those that gauge the financial losses from fraud. These can be further divided between detected and estimated.

The most common and the most flawed indicators of levels of fraud are detected frauds. These are usually presented as the number of frauds detected and the losses from each. Some organisations might only present one or the other. Many organisations keep statistics illustrating their detected frauds (this is at least better than some organisations, which don't even compile statistics on detected losses). As demonstrated above, these do not offer a realistic measure of the actual size of the problem because the vast majority of frauds are usually undetected. Understandably, many organisations that keep these statistics do not publish them. It is generally in the public sector where one can find this type of data published, for reasons of public accountability and transparency.

In the UK, HM Treasury Department used to conduct an annual survey among Government Departments and other central public bodies of detected internal fraud (amongst other issues related to fraud).[8] In the last survey, conducted in 2008–9, of the 45 bodies that responded, 20 entered a nil return. These are bodies with budgets of millions and billions of pounds employing hundreds and thousands of staff. Even among those that detected fraud, of the 25 who did report it there were a total of 1,320 cases amounting to just over £4.2 million.[9] This is in reality likely to be the tip of the iceberg, because the vast majority of frauds go undetected.

Overseas aid is an area of expenditure well known for the risk of fraud and corruption. Many countries who give aid do not publish statistics on the extent of fraud. One of the few is Australia. AusAID is the body responsible and its approach to fraud is laid out in its Fraud Policy Statement and figures are given in its annual Fraud Fact Sheet.[10] During 2010–11 125 cases of alleged, suspected or detected fraud were reported to AusAID. In addition, a further 24 potential instances were reported during the year, but were found not to have involved fraud or not to have involved AusAID. It is likely that, as the remaining active cases are further investigated, some additional cases will be found not to have involved fraud and/or AusAID. AusAID estimates that the amount involved in the 125 2010–11 cases is AUD $1.6m. Of this amount, AUD $400,000 had been recovered or prevented from being lost and the potential net loss to AusAID is therefore estimated to be approximately AUD $1.26m. This represents 0.028 per cent of the $4.498 billion appropriated to AusAID in 2010–11, a percentage consistent with previous years (0.02 per cent). Given the risk of fraud in this area, this is likely to under-estimate the true extent of fraud in this area.

More realistic measures are those which seek to gauge the extent of fraud beyond the detected frauds. Some of these surveys are, however, based upon unsound methodologies, as they ask the respondent to guess the size of the fraud problem in their organisation. By their very methodology, therefore, they are not truly accurate. The most salient example of this type of report is the ACFE Report to the Nation, which is regularly published. Prior to the 2010 report it focused upon the USA, but this report now provides a global picture. ACFE ask respondents to estimate the losses to fraud their organisation suffers as a percentage. In the 2012 report the median response was 5 per cent which if translated across the world would amount to $3.5 trillion.[11] Clearly one has to be careful of research based upon estimates, although the 5 per cent figure is similar to the authors' estimate which will be shortly discussed.

The most accurate measures of fraud are fraud loss measurement exercises. This will be the subject of much more depth in Chapter 5. The principles of these measures are focusing upon a particular type of transaction, such as procurement expenditure, then identifying a statistically valid sample of transactions, investigating them to a higher standard than normal auditing processes to identify whether they are fraudulent or not. From this it is possible to identify the numbers of frauds (Fraud Frequency Rate – FFR) and losses (Percentage Loss Rate – PLR) to a particular level of statistical confidence.[12]

The authors (along with Graham Brooks) have assessed 203 exercises to accurately measure fraud and error losses, covering 32 different types of expenditure totalling almost £800 billion, in 44 organisations from nine countries. Including the types of expenditure where exercises have been repeated, they have examined a total of expenditure valued at £5 trillion, sterling equivalent. From this we found the PLR was found to be between 0.12 and 10.60 per cent with an average PLR of 5.67 per cent as shown in Figure 2.3. To further analyse this, the authors broke this down into exercises showing less than 3 per cent, 3 to 8 per cent and over 8 per cent. As Figure 2.4 illustrates, around 70 per cent of the exercises

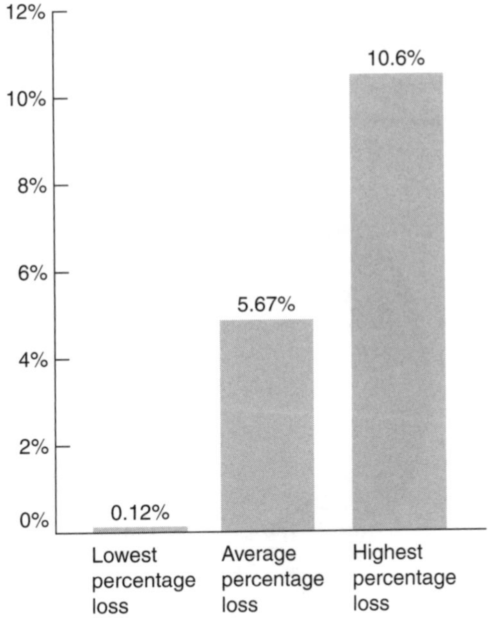

Figure 2.3 Average Percentage Losses to Fraud and Error

showed PLR figures of more than 3 per cent with a quarter with a PLR over 8 per cent.[13]

The first report on the financial cost of fraud also assessed FFR. The range of FFR was found to be between 0.47 and 9.6 per cent, with an average FFR of 4.28 per cent as shown in Figure 2.5. There was a much more common grouping on this criterion with 90 per cent of exercises assessed recording a FFR of 3 to 8 per cent, and only 1.67 per cent recording over 8 per cent as shown in Figure 2.6. Given the dominance of the 3 to 8 per cent this may suggest that a fraud and error rate of between 3 to 8 per cent is the norm.[14]

A significant finding was that organisations that repeated the fraud measurement exercises tended to a show a reduction in the PLR. The average PLR when first measured has been found to be 5.40 per cent; the average PLR when last measured was found to be 4.61 per cent as shown in Figure 2.7. This represents an average reduction of just under 15 per cent. The authors would argue that once an organisation discovers an accurate measure of fraud losses this acts as an incentive and spur

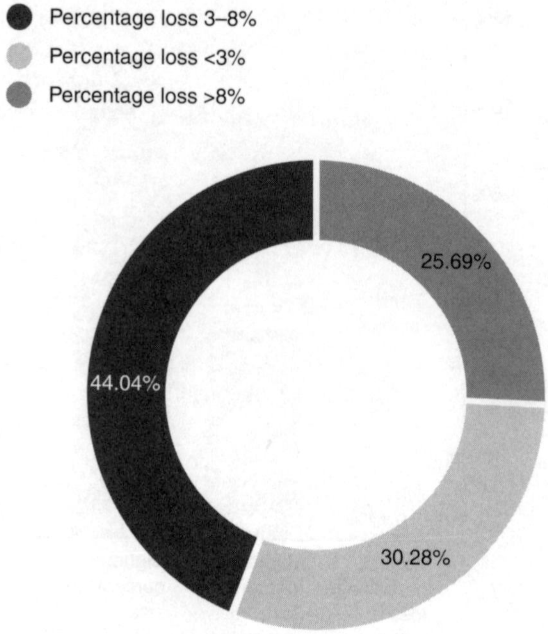

Figure 2.4 Percentage Losses by Amount

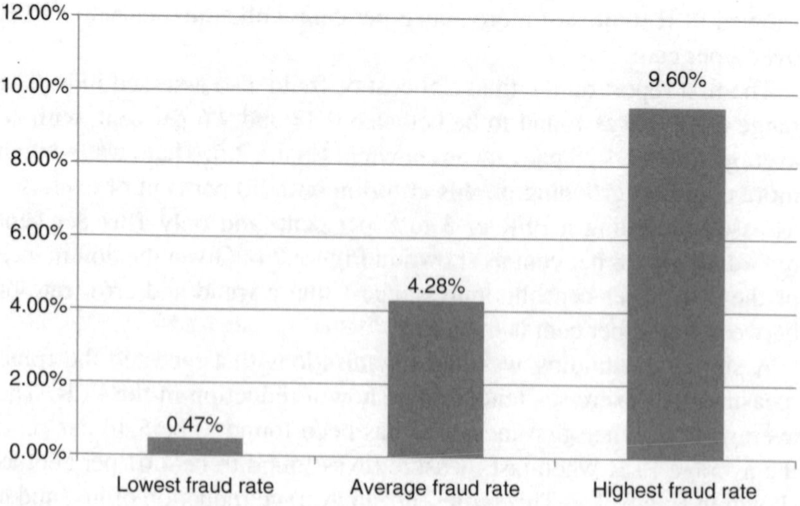

Figure 2.5 Average Fraud Frequency Rates

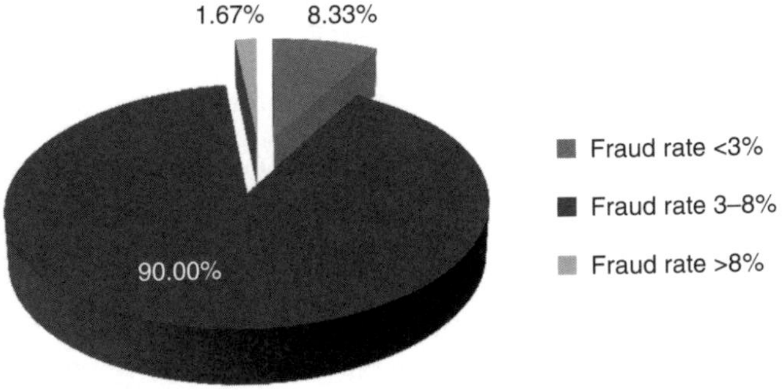

Figure 2.6 Fraud Frequency Rates by Amount

to introduce measures to reduce fraud losses. It also shows that fraud can be reduced and that in many organisations a saving of 15 per cent of fraud losses would amount to a significant sum of money. This book will also show later how savings of 40 per cent are not unreasonable to achieve.

If these figures are extrapolated globally the costs of fraud would amount to £2.74 trillion or the equivalent cost of healthcare worldwide for a year or the combined GDP of the UK and France.

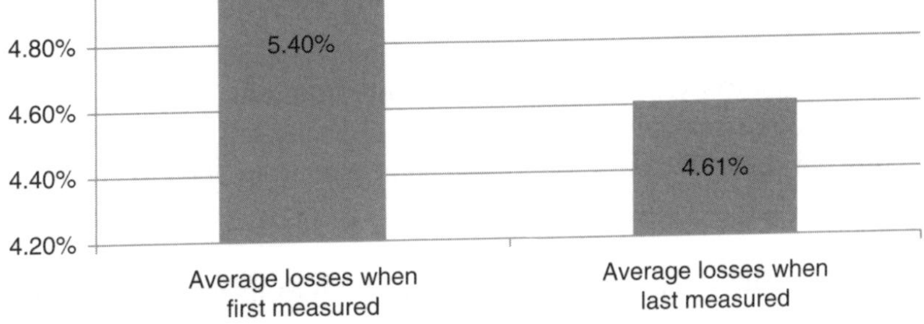

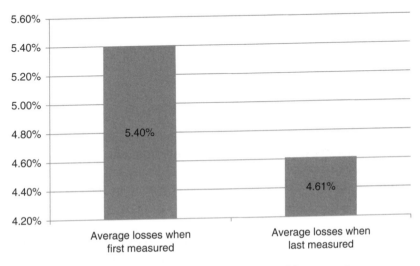

Figure 2.7 Average Losses Compared from First to Last Measurement

Key Facts

The average percentage loss rate was found to be 5.67 per cent.

Only just under a third of organisations had a percentage loss rate less than 3 per cent.

A quarter of organisations had a percentage loss rate of 8 per cent or more.

The average fraud frequency rate was found to be 4.28 per cent.

Fraud measurement encourages action to reduce losses with the average percentage loss rate reducing from 5.4 per cent on the first time to 4.61 per cent on the second.

This research would suggest an average organisation's losses from fraud (and error) to be around 5 per cent. However, with the appropriate counter-fraud strategy in place it could be lower than 1 per cent. Conversely without the appropriate strategy in place it could be much higher. Chapter 5 will highlight the importance and principles of measuring fraud accurately. This is the foundation of any effective counter-fraud strategy. Not to do so is like a doctor prescribing a cancer treatment without having undertaken appropriate tests to gauge the type and extent of the cancer. To tackle the problem of fraud it is necessary to know the size, extent and nature of the problem. That is why accurate fraud measurement is so important. Now the size of the problem has been gauged in an organisation it would be useful to look at recent trends in fraud to assess if it is becoming a greater risk.

2.4 TRENDS IN FRAUD

The ideal way to plot trends in fraud would be to plot the fraud risk measurement exercises described above over time. It is possible to do this for some areas of Federal expenditure in the USA. The graph in Figure 2.8 shows the error rate (fraud and error) from 2004 to 2009 and shows a small decline in the mid noughties before a rise towards the end.

However, this is a narrow area of expenditure in the public sector in one country. It is not yet possible to secure such data across a wider range of public and private bodies, year by year, of a big enough sample,

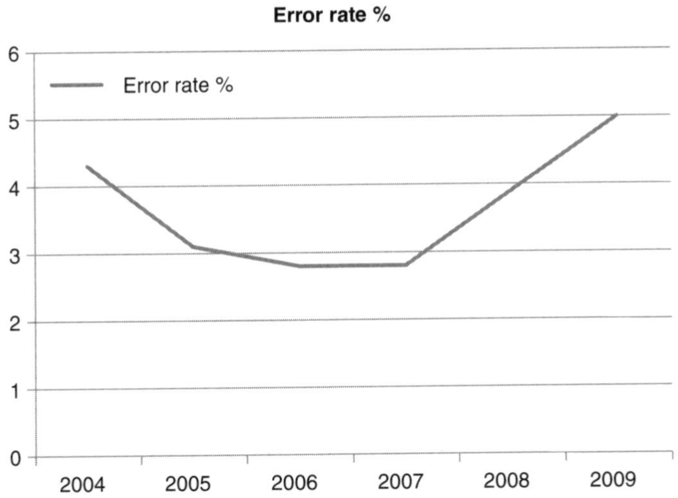

Figure 2.8 Error Rate by Percentage in US Bodies Covered by Improper Payments Legislation[15]

because of the rarity of FLM. Therefore one is left with using less reliable measures of fraud to plot trends. In the introduction to this book it was shown how some of the factors associated with increased risk of fraud have become more prevalent since the post-financial crisis recession from 2007 onwards. There are a number of measures from the USA and the UK which can be used to illustrate the rise in fraud during this period. The first is from England and Wales and the annual British Crime Survey. This is a survey of around 25,000 households which seeks information on their crime victimization. The graph in Figure 2.9 shows that while total crime has fallen during the recession (which is the opposite to what is normally expected), the percentage of the population who have experienced the unauthorised use of their plastic card has gone up from 3.4 per cent in 2005–6 to 6.4 per cent in 2009–10 – a near doubling of this crime – and then fallen back to 5.2 per cent in 2010–11. Most credit card fraud is perpetrated by career and occasional fraudsters. It provides evidence of an upward trend for this type of fraud in England and Wales during the last five years, with a slight decrease in the most recent statistics.[16]

In the UK there are also some 'fraud barometers' which give a rough indication of trends in fraud, particularly internal fraud. The KPMG Fraud Barometer plots the number of cases in the courts relating to

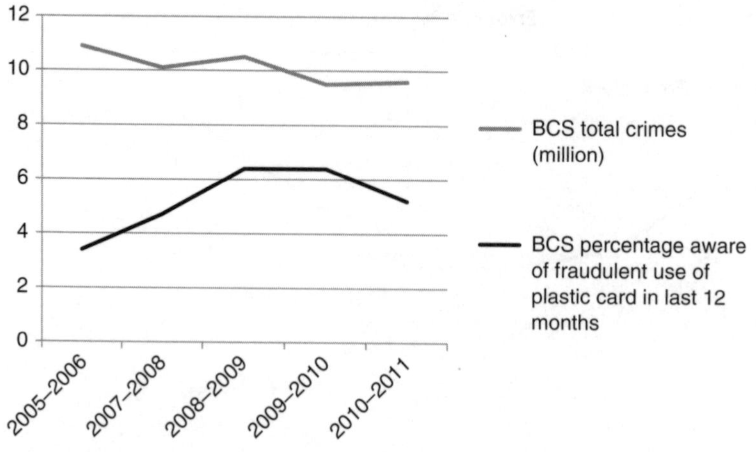

Note: The question relating to plastic card unauthorised use was removed in 2006–7.

Figure 2.9 Comparing the Rate of Credit Card Fraud to Total Crime in England and Wales

fraud of at least £100,000, whereas the BDO Fraud Track does so for cases over £50,000. The KPMG barometer shows the number of cases of fraud in 2007 to be 198 rising to 314 in 2010 and then back to 251 in 2011. The value, however, had risen from just over £1 billion to over £3.5 billion in 2011.[17] The BDO Fraud Track dropped from £1.3 billion to £1 billion, but then jumped to over £2 billion during the period up to 2009. These are best taken as barometers of trends in fraud and what they show is a substantial rise from 2007 to 2009/10 (see Figure 2.10).[18]

The final illustration of trends in fraud in the UK is the National Fraud Authority's annual fraud indicator (see Figure 2.11). This uses a basket of measures to estimate the costs of fraud to the UK economy. The methodology has changed each year and in reality it represents a more accurate grasp of the totality of fraud each year. Nevertheless from 2009 to 2011 the measure has gone from just over £30 billion to £73 billion.[19]

In the USA the complexities of multiple state and Federal enforcement bodies make a national picture of trends in fraud even more difficult. However, the FBI's Uniform Crime Reports (UCR) provide a basic barometer for trends in fraud and embezzlement across the USA. Figure 2.12 shows this data from 2000 and shows an upward trend over the period for both types of offences.

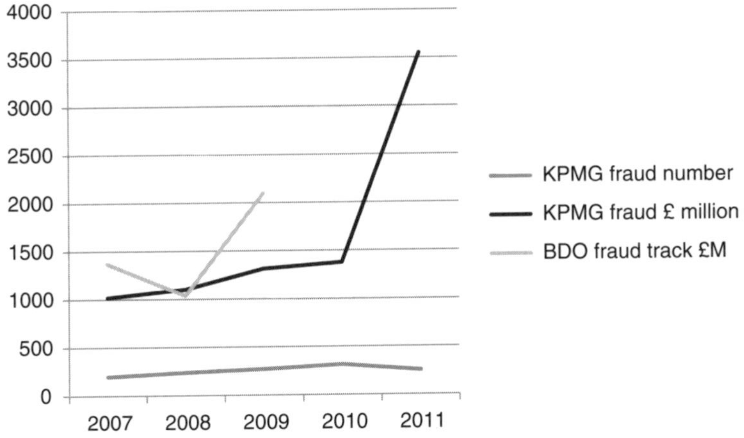

Note: BDO uses a slightly different year-to-year point to KPMG
2010 data were not published.

Figure 2.10 The KPMG UK Fraud Barometer/BDO Fraud Track 2007–2011

There are two other measures which are regularly used and which can provide insights into trends in fraud in the USA. The first is from the Federal Trade Commission's Consumer Sentinel Network and covers the number of complaints from consumers relating to frauds and scams. The most common include prize/lottery scams, shop-at-home frauds, advanced fee frauds etc. As these types of frauds are generally

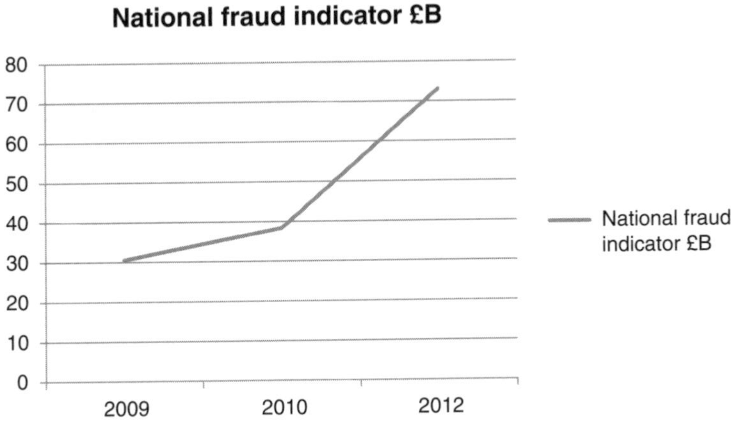

Figure 2.11 The National Fraud Authority's UK Annual Fraud Indicator

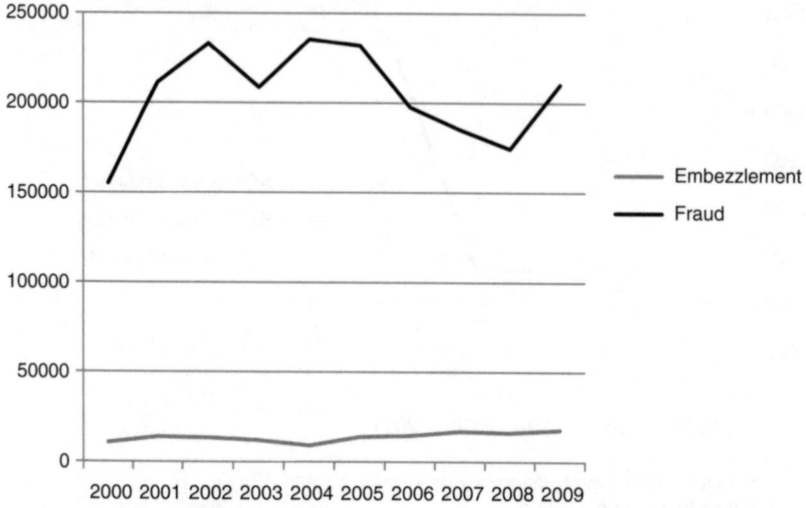

Figure 2.12 US Uniform Crime Reports for Fraud and Embezzlement 2000–2009[20]

perpetrated by organised fraudsters it provides some useful data on the extent and strength of their activity. The graph in Figure 2.13 shows more than a doubling of the number of complaints from 2003 to 2010, and a marked increase from 2006, both domestically in the USA and from frauds perpetrated from other countries.[21]

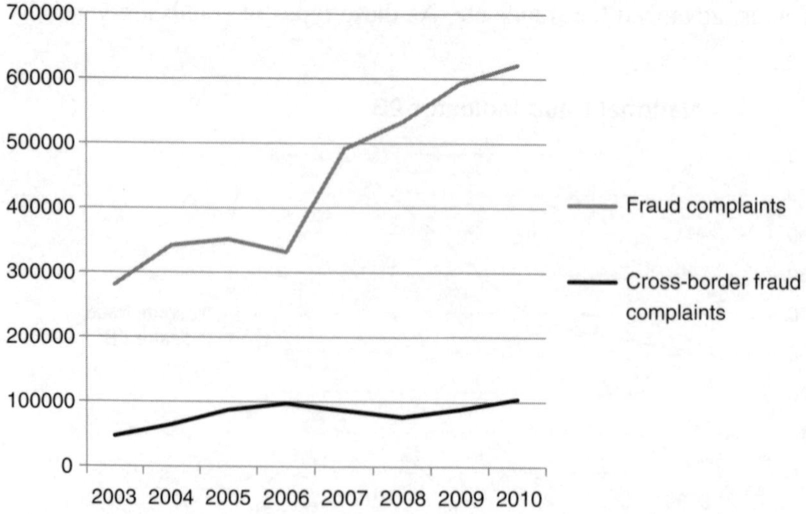

Figure 2.13 US Federal Trade Commission Fraud Complaints 2003–2010

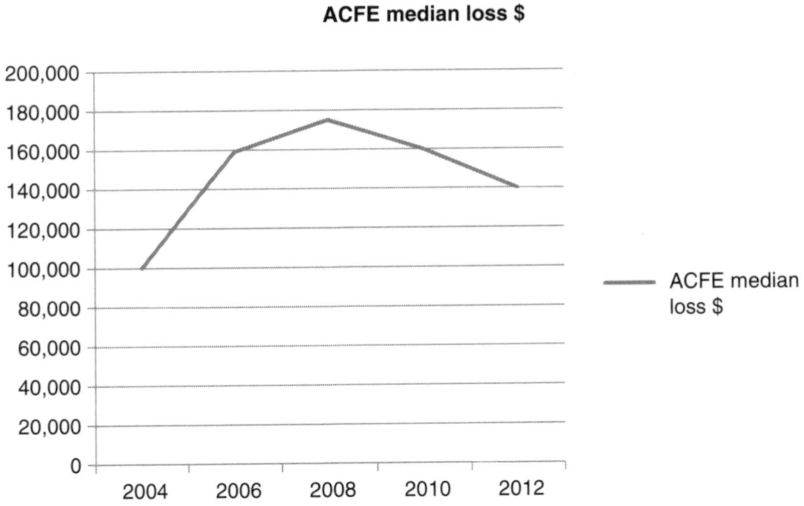

Figure 2.14 ACFE Median Loss Per Organisation 2004–12

To gauge trends in internal fraud in the USA the best longitudinal source is the ACFE Report to the Nation. The best available data from these surveys to illustrate trends are the median loss of fraud per organisation (see Figure 2.14). This shows an increase from $100,000 in 2004 to $175,000 in 2008 and then back to $140,000 in 2012. However, the 2010 and 2012 figures are based upon global data, whereas the others are based only upon the USA. Nevertheless the trend in the amount lost to occupational fraud from 2004 onwards has been upwards.

The above discussion shows – bearing the weaknesses of each measure in mind – that there is evidence in both England and Wales and the USA of an increase in both internal fraud and frauds perpetrated against the public during the latter half of the noughties. This latter type of fraud is important in distinguishing the activity of organised fraudsters. This, in England and Wales, can also be juxtaposed against declining levels of crime in general. This is therefore evidence that organisations need to be on their guard even more in the current climate with the rise in fraud which is taking place and the greater risk it poses.

2.5 THE IMPACT OF FRAUD

There is a general perception amongst many that fraud is a victimless crime. Even many organisations regularly targeted with fraud often dismiss the impact because they consider losses to be small and, for any that do transpire, the costs can be passed on to someone else. However, the discussion above has shown that the real fraud losses are more than the detected losses. There is a financial loss to an organisation and – unless they are accurately measuring it – it will be more than they think. At its most devastating, fraud can destroy an organisation. Consider the following names: Barings Bank, Enron and Worldcom. All of these were destroyed by fraud. Some developed fraudulent cultures driven from the top, such as Enron, others were destroyed by one fraud perpetrated alone, such as Nick Leeson's destruction of Barings Bank.[22]

There are many organisations who may not be destroyed by fraud, but who suffer devastating consequences as a result of fraud. This can occur in terms of losses from fraud, or penalties for not tackling fraud (corruption). Possibly the biggest fraud perpetrated against an organisation, which didn't destroy it, were the trades by a rogue trader within Société Générale, which amounted to €4.9 billion.[23] The German company Siemens, as a result of corrupt practices, received fines and costs in the USA amounting to $2.5 billion.[24] The British firm BAE Systems was also fined £286 million in the USA for similar problems.[25] There are also many Small and Medium Enterprises (SMEs) which operate on very tight budgets, and a major fraud can result in serious damage to them. Evidence from America shows the median losses are higher in organisations employing fewer than 100 employees than they are in larger ones. For example for the former it was $150,000 compared to $84,000 in those employing 10,000+.[26] There is therefore a simple imperative to tackle fraud to reduce the potential financial impact and to avoid the ultimate consequences of disappearing altogether. There are other compelling reasons too.

2.5.1 Fraud Leads to More Fraud

Wilson and Kelling have famously argued that broken windows lead to more broken windows. This has spawned a multiplicity of attempts that seek to enhance security via dealing with these trivial acts – so called zero tolerance policing.[27] These same signals of social decay can also be applied to acts of dishonesty. If a culture begins to emerge where such behaviour is tolerated, it is, in the authors' view, likely to lead to more fraud. Therefore if an organisation is suffering from fraud – which it might perceive to be too low to warrant action – this can send out a message that fraud is acceptable. Some will also see others getting away with it and think it's only fair for them to do so as well. The impact of fraud, if not effectively tackled, can therefore lead to more fraud. That is why it's vital to pursue zero tolerance. Developing an anti-fraud culture as part of that is very important, and this will be returned to in Chapter 6.

2.5.2 Psychological and Health Impacts

In many cases of fraud against organisations employees affected (who have not perpetrated the fraud) generally suffer no financial impact. In small and medium-sized organisations – so-called SMEs – the impact is more likely to damage the sustainability of the organisation. Some staff can become affected by this and more so if they have a financial stake in the body or were in a position where they feel they were partly responsible. This can culminate in psychological impacts such as stress, anger and anxiety, not to mention physical and health problems. The Centre for Counter Fraud Studies published a *vox populi* of accounts of victims, some of which were owners/co-owners of SMEs.[28] The three extracts below illustrate the impact of fraud on SME owners/co-owners. Mike and Steve had purchased a company and subsequently found it was riddled with fraud and corruption, which culminated in losses of £8 million.

> Er, yeah, I would say with me, yes. **I've been mentally to the brink a couple of times**. Yeah. So ... I've always thought I'm pretty strong but, you know, um, er, it's when you have to carry the baggage of your own family, that's, that's difficult (Mike, multiple fraud victim)

> Yeah. It's, it's when your son says to you ... 11 year old son says to you, um, don't worry dad, I'll buy mum's Christmas present this year. I mean, er ... [breaks off] (Steve, multiple fraud victim).

Peter ran a small business and employed an accountant who subsequently defrauded his business of £80,000. One of the many effects included:

> But if you want to see class A psoriasis which I didn't have before ... and if there is, um, any relationship as they say there is between stress and psoriasis (Peter, small business victim).

Bernard had run a small niche manufacturing company and employed a new chief executive to grow the company. She turned out to be corrupt and destroyed his company losing him over £300,000. He described the impact.

> Our lawyer considers that she's done this several times before. The whole way the documentation, the finesse, the extra elegant trills ... Very elegant. Why doesn't she put her energy into being effective and make profit for people? That's what makes me so sick. No, she's got greed going all over her, and I don't know, what do you say? I mean it's all gone. It's all gone. I mean your, your health ... it's like divorce. 15 months ... absolute shit. If my, my ... if, if ... I tell you, if ... **without my wife I'd have gone under**. She just kept on pulling through (Bernard, small business fraud victim).

2.5.3 Reputation

Fraud can also seriously damage the reputation of an organisation. Identity theft for individuals is an increasing risk to society; organisations can also suffer from this problem. A survey of small businesses in the UK in 2009 found 6 per cent had experienced corporate identity theft.[29] When identities are stolen to perpetrate crimes this can seriously damage the reputation of an organisation. Frauds against an organisation can also damage the reputation for competence of some bodies if they reach the public domain. Indeed, such is the damage which many perceive can be done, they refuse to consider criminal prosecutions which would mean it would enter the public domain. In one case one of the authors was involved in investigating a £50 million fraud in a bank. Such was the fear of bad publicity the investigation was purely about finding out what had happened and seeking to secure some of the money back. Not taking fraud seriously, turning a blind eye or placing one's head in the sand can all be equally disastrous for an organisation. Arthur Andersen was once one of the leading accountancy, audit and consultancy firms. Its failure to effectively audit Enron and the relationships it established with them destroyed its reputation when the Enron scandal broke, culminating in the collapse of Arthur Andersen.[30]

2.5.4 Change in Behaviour

The impact of fraud can also be to change the behaviour of those who have suffered from the fraud. This can affect how many organisations do business, impacting upon their potential profitability. Research on individual victims of fraud has found that some victims who experience fraud through online purchasing are less likely to use that facility again. One can apply the same logic to an organisation. For example, if fraud is exposed in the online purchasing arrangements of a company, consumers may be less likely to trust the website and, as a consequence, that may affect the business. A charity which experiences fraud may be less likely to receive donations. For all these reasons it is essential to counter fraud.

2.6 CONCLUSION

This chapter has considered the problem of fraud. It began by defining it, illustrating some of the legal definitions and then some of the wide variety of ways in which fraud is perpetrated. The chapter then went on to consider the extent of fraud and showed that it would be normal to expect a loss rate of 5 per cent based upon fraud loss measurement exercises. Some of the limited data on trends in fraud in the USA and UK were then explored to reveal an upward trend in the extent of fraud. Finally this chapter considered the impact of fraud upon an organisation. It would now seem natural to consider who perpetrates fraud and why, and the cultural factors, amongst others, which influence it.

FURTHER READING

ACFE (2012) *Report to the Nation on Occupational Fraud and Abuse*. Austin: ACFE.

Farrell, S., Yeo, N. and Ladenburg, G. (2007) *Blackstone's Guide to the Fraud Act 2006*. Oxford: Oxford University Press.

Gee, J., Button, M. and Brooks, G. (2010a) *The Financial Cost of Public Sector Fraud*. London: MacIntyre Hudson/CCFS.

END NOTES

1. ACFE (2010) *Report to the Nation on Occupational Fraud and Abuse*. Austin: ACFE.
2. Wells, J.T. (1997) *Occupational Fraud and Abuse*. Dexter (MI): Obsidian, p. 2.
3. Cited at European Healthcare Fraud and Corruption Network (n.d.) *What is Fraud and Corruption*. Retrieved on 5 August 2011 from http://www.ehfcn.org/fraud-corruption/.
4. See Farrell, S., Yeo, N. and Ladenburg, G. (2007) *Blackstone's Guide to the Fraud Act 2006*. Oxford: Oxford University Press.
5. Ibid.
6. Asian Development Bank (n.d.) *Definitions of Corruption*. Retrieved 5 August 2011 from http://www.adb.org/documents/policies/anticorruption/anticorrupt300.asp.

7. PKF (2012) *The 'Bottom 10 Frauds of 2011'*. Retrieved 1 August 2012 from http://www.pkf.co.uk/pkf/news/press_release/the_%E2%80%98bottom_10%E2%80%99_frauds_of_2011&goto=5.
8. See HM Treasury (2005), Fraud Report 2004–05 An Analysis of Reported Fraud in Government Departments, London, HM Treasury; HM Treasury (2006), Fraud Report 2005–06 An Analysis of Reported Fraud in Government Departments, London, HM Treasury; HM Treasury (2007), Fraud Report 2006–07 An Analysis of Reported Fraud in Government Departments, London, HM Treasury; HM Treasury (2008), Fraud Report 2007–08 An Analysis of Reported Fraud in Government Departments, London, HM Treasury.
9. HM Treasury (2008) op. cit.
10. AusAID (2011) *Fraud Control at AusAID*. Retrieved 12 October 2011 from http://www.ausaid.gov.au/publications/pubout.cfm?ID=7618_6876_7414_705_9251&Type=.
11. ACFE (2012) *Report to the Nations on Occupational Fraud and Abuse 2012 Global Study*. Austin: ACFE.
12. See Gee, J., Button, M. and Brooks, G. (2010a) *The Financial Cost of Public Sector Fraud*. London: MacIntyre Hudson/CCFS; Gee, J., Button, M. and Brooks, G. (2010b) *The Financial Cost of Healthcare Fraud*. London: MacIntyre Hudson/CCFS; and Gee, J., Button, M. and Brooks, G. (2009) *The Financial Cost of Fraud*. London: MacIntyre Hudson/CCFS.
13. Gee, J., Button, M. and Brooks, G. (2011) *The Financial Cost of Fraud. What the data from around the world shows*. London: PKF/CCFS.
14. Gee, J., Button, M. and Brooks, G. (2010a) op. cit.
15. Hatch, G. and McMurty, V.A. (2010) *Improper Payments Act of 2002: Background, Information and Assessment. Congressional Research Service*. Retrieved 24 July 2012 from http://www.policyarchive.org/handle/10207/bitstreams/18930.pdf, p. 9.
16. Chaplin, R., Flatley, J. and Smith, K. (2011) Crime in England and Wales 2010–11. Retrieved 5 August 2011 from http://www.homeoffice.gov.uk/publications/science-research-statistics/research-statistics/crime-research/hosb1011/hosb1011?view=Binary.
17. KPMG (2011) *KPMG Forensic Fraud Barometer 2010*. Retrieved 5 August 2011 from http://www.yhff.co.uk/KPMG%20FB%20Jan%202010.pdf. KPMG (2010) KPMG Fraud Barometer 2009. Retrieved 5 August 2011 from http://www.yhff.co.uk/Fraud%20Barometer%20-%20Feb%202009%20_2_.pdf. KPMG (2012) Boom Time for Fraudsters as 'Austerity Bites'. Retrieved 12 April 2012 from http://www.kpmg.com/uk/en/issuesandinsights/articlespublications/newsreleases/pages/fraud-barometer-boom-time-for-fraudsters-as-austerity-bites.aspx.
18. Ibid.
19. National Fraud Authority (2012) *Annual Fraud Indicator*. London: NFA; National Fraud Authority (2011) *Annual Fraud Indicator*. London: NFA; National Fraud Authority (2010) *Annual Fraud Indicator*. London: NFA.
20. Payne, B. (2013) *White Collar Crime*. Thousand Oaks (CA): Sage, p. 35.
21. Consumer Sentinel Network (2011) *Cross-Border Fraud Complaints January–December 2010*. Retrieved 5 August 2011 from http://www.ftc.gov/sentinel/reports/annual-crossborder-reports/crossborder-cy2010.pdf; Consumer Sentinel (2008) *Cross-Border Fraud Complaints January–December 2007*. Retrieved 5

August 2011 from http://www.ftc.gov/sentinel/reports/annual-crossborder-reports/crossborder-cy2007.pdf.
22. See McLean, B. and Elkind, P. (2004) *The Smartest Guys in the Room*. New York: Penguin; and Leeson, N. (1996) *Rogue Trader*. London: Little Brown.
23. Walsh, F. and Gow, D. (2008) Société Générale Uncovers £3.7 billion fraud by Rogue Trader. Retrieved 5 August 2011 from http://www.guardian.co.uk/business/2008/jan/24/creditcrunch.banking.
24. Gow, D. (2008) *Record US Fine Ends Siemens Bribery Scandal*. Retrieved 5 August 2011 from http://www.guardian.co.uk/business/2008/dec/16/regulation-siemens-scandal-bribery.
25. BBC News (2010) *BAE Systems Handed £286 Million Fines in UK and US*. Retrieved 5 August 2011 from http://news.bbc.co.uk/1/hi/8500535.stm.
26. ACFE (2010) op. cit., p. 30.
27. Wilson, J.Q. and Kelling, G.L. (1982) Broken Windows: The Police and Neighbourhood Safety. *The Atlantic Monthly*, March, pp. 29–38.
28. Button, M., Gee, J., Lewis, C. and Tapley, J. (2010) *The Human Cost of Fraud: A Vox Populi*. London: MacIntyre Hudson/CCFS.
29. Federation of Small Businesses (2009) *Inhibiting Enterprise: Fraud and Online Crime Against Small Businesses*. London: Federation of Small Businesses.
30. Hamilton, S. and Micklethwait, A. (2006) *Greed and Corporate Failure*. Basingstoke: Palgrave, pp. 55–56.

3

The Fraudster and the Culture of Fraud

3.1 INTRODUCTION

In this chapter the fraudster and the culture of fraud are considered. It is important to understand why people turn to fraud and what factors influence this. There is not a huge literature on this subject, but there is a growing base. The chapter will therefore begin by examining research on fraudsters, reviewing different types of them and the factors which influence why they become fraudsters. This will include an overview of some of the research which profiles occupational fraudsters, as well as Cressey's famous fraud triangle which seeks to explain the actions of individual fraudsters. The cultural influences at both a national and organisational level are also important, and this chapter will move on to examine some of the differences which exist, as well as some of the factors which influence such cultures.

3.2 UNDERSTANDING THE FRAUDSTER

It would be useful to begin with an examination of research on fraudsters. Understanding their motives, rationalisation, and techniques all aid the counter-fraud professional in tailoring their response. As Sun Tzu in *The Art of War* argued, 'If you know your enemy and know yourself you need not fear the results of a hundred battles.'[1] Practitioners, however, are often surprised to learn that in the vast field of criminology there has not been a significant amount of research on the criminals themselves, how they committed their crimes, and their motivations for doing so. Common sense would suggest that getting inside the minds of criminals would greatly aid the battle against them. However, despite the gaps, there is a thin but growing body of research on different types of criminals – including fraudsters – which is beginning to shed light on their modus operandi and motivations at a general level and, in particular, to fraud. Typologies of fraudsters are rare, but drawing upon a number of studies of them, four 'ideal' types of fraudster can be identified:[2]

Career fraudsters – These are malefactors whose primary motive and purpose is to commit fraud (as well as possibly other types of crime). For internal fraud they will seek to secure employment with an organisation for the purpose of spotting opportunities to commit fraud. Some career fraudsters operate externally, targeting organisations or the public with scams; others work within organisations. Some, such as Frank Abagnale, may practise as fraudsters for a period of time and, when caught, change their ways. The other notable fraudster in this category listed below is Bernie Madoff.

Examples

Probably the most famous career fraudster is Frank Abagnale who, in the USA during the 1960s, perpetrated a variety of frauds including cashing several million dollars of bad cheques, impersonating a pilot and faking qualifications to secure jobs, to name a few. His 'career' was turned into the movie 'Catch Me if you Can', starring Leonardo Di Caprio. Eventually he was caught and began to help the FBI to counter fraud. He now runs a successful counter-fraud business, Abagnale and Associates.[3]

Another good example is Bernie Madoff who in March 2009 pleaded guilty to running the world's largest ever Ponzi scheme (investment fraud). This had involved thousands of investors and some $65 billion. Madoff had run this for many years and it had involved serial fabrication of false investments and returns. He was sentenced to 150 years' jail for this crime.[4]

Occasional fraudster – These are people who generally are law-abiding, but who have a history of occasional dishonesty. The important difference is that they do not embark with the primary objective of committing fraud. They are, however, likely in the right circumstances to engage in fraudulent behaviour. There are examples of many employees with a history of fraud/dishonesty who are sacked and then secure another job, not with the primary purpose of pursuing more fraud; however, opportunities may arise and because of their character they exploit them. Such a fraudster might commit an external fraud, such as an insurance fraud, social security fraud etc. Again, they may not take out an insurance policy with the purpose of committing fraud, but an opportunity arises for them to exploit it.

Examples

Major Charles Ingram rose to fame when he successfully won the £1 million prize in the television game show 'Who Wants to be Millionaire', but on suspicions of cheating the payment was suspended. Following an investigation his wife, an accomplice – Tecwen Whittock – and he were charged with deception-related offences, found guilty and given suspended prison sentences.[5] They all still maintain their innocence despite the conviction. However, not long after this incident in 2003 he was given a conditional discharge after being found guilty of a £30,000 fraudulent insurance claim.[6]

Another example is a financial director of a large advertising agency who stole £2 million. She spent the money on a Spanish villa, a Ferrari, a BMW, and six Porsches amongst many other luxury items. Such was the financial impact of the fraud on her firm that staff were made redundant while she carried on embezzling. In her previous job she had also perpetrated a fraud of £25,000 and been caught and convicted in the criminal courts. She hid this conviction from her next employers and set about fraud on an even grander scale.[7]

Fallen fraudster – The third type of fraudster is the fallen fraudster. These are people who are law-abiding with no history of prior fraud/dishonesty but, because of personal circumstance married with opportunity, engage in fraud. Most internal fraudsters fit into this category. The ACFE's 2012 report to the nation found that only 6 per cent of the fraudsters in their sample had prior convictions for fraud-related offences.[8]

Examples

There are many examples of 'fallen fraudsters'. Paul Hopes is typical of many. An accountant who had worked for a major toy retailer for over 20 years with no major blemishes on his record, between 2006 and 2008 he embarked upon a fraud amounting to £3.6 million against his employer. He had spent the money on prostitutes, drugs, and expensive cars, even buying a house for a regular prostitute. The addiction to sex, drugs, and cars combined with greed had driven him to perpetrate fraud. He was sentenced to seven years' imprisonment.[9]

The 'ordinary Joe' fraudster – The final category of fraudster could be called the 'ordinary Joe fraudster'. This is essentially most people, and is based upon the hypothesis that most people, in the right circumstances, will be prepared to engage in a little dishonesty, particularly if they see others doing it and getting away with it. This is based upon the research of Mazar, Ariely et al. on dishonesty. In various experiments to test the potential to engage in dishonest acts, where participants thought they would get away with cheating, or were encouraged to cheat by an actor, the rates of cheating rose significantly in comparison to the control group.[10] Thus for all organisations there is a risk that most staff may engage in minor acts of dishonesty.

3.2.1 Profiling Fraudsters

There is much interest in the subject of offender profiling, where the key characteristics of offenders are identified with the aim of enabling better prevention and detection of fraud. There have been a number of attempts to profile fraudsters. These have tended to focus upon internal/occupational frauds, which, as shown above, are generally committed by 'fallen fraudsters'. Table 3.1 below profiles the characteristics from KPMG,[11] ACFE,[12] and Bushman and Werle.[13] The latter also included external fraudsters in their analysis. The ACFE study is based upon global returns and KPMG's on returns from Europe, the Middle East, and

Table 3.1 Comparing the Profiles of Occupational Fraudsters

	KPMG 2007	ACFE 2010	Bushman and Werle
Gender	Male – 85%	Male – 82%	Male – 87%
Age	36–55 – 70%	36–50 – 53%	31–50 – 71%
Employment	+6 Years – 50%	+6 Years – 49%	
Top Management	66%	58%	18%

Africa. The ACFE research, which is broken down into regions, shows substantial differences between the regions, which will be explored later.

The KPMG research was based upon 360 cases of fraud from 700 investigations in their Europe, Middle East, and Africa regions. Their profile of a typical fraudster was a male (85 per cent), who was middle-aged (between 36 and 55) (70 per cent), committing a fraud against their own employer (89 per cent), acting alone (68 per cent), for whom over 50 per cent had worked for at least six years. Most disturbingly two thirds of all primary perpetrators were from top management. The ACFE study showed similar characteristics: male, six years plus employment, but not quite as many senior managers and not as strongly middle-aged. The research from Bushman and Werle was based upon a global survey of 5,500 companies, where respondents were asked to report in depth two cases of economic crime. The mixture of internal and external may explain why the top management category is significantly different from the other two surveys as well as the broader range of crimes considered: frauds, corruption and bribery, money laundering, insider dealing, and counterfeiting. Otherwise the profile of the offenders was similar to KPMG and ACFE.

The ACFE research, however, does illustrate significant regional differences. They found men accounting for over 80 per cent of fraudsters in Europe, Asia, and Central/South America/Caribbean. However, in the USA and Canada women accounted for over 40 per cent, and in Oceania and Africa 32 per cent and 24 per cent respectively. The dominance of senior managers perpetrating fraud also varied. In Oceania it was 60 per cent and in Asia, Europe, and Central/South America/Caribbean they accounted for around two thirds of frauds, whereas in the USA, Canada, and Africa it was just over half. This illustrates that, when considering fraud from a global perspective, it is important not to stereotype based upon one's own region.

Key Facts

The typical profile of an internal fraudster is:

No prior history of fraud or dishonesty
Male (not as dominant in North America)
Middle Aged (mid 30s to early 50s)
Employed six years plus
Senior manager plus

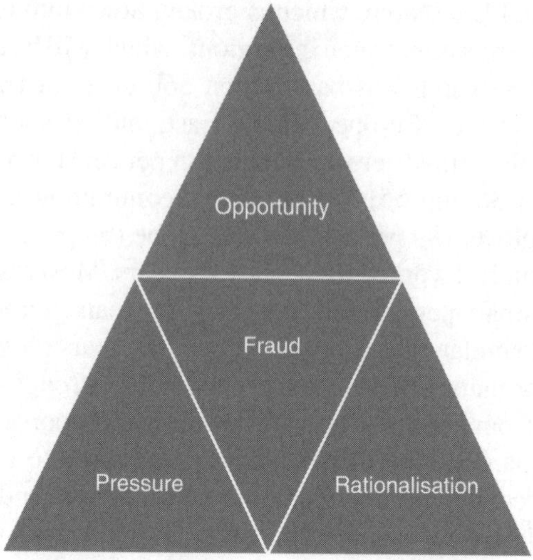

Figure 3.1 Cressey's Fraud Triangle

Research by CIFAS/CIPD[14] (n.d.) has also profiled the fraudster who leaks compromising personal data for the purposes of identity fraud. Here the fraudster is generally much younger (under 25), male, employed full-time, employed for less than a year, in a junior non-management role, low-paid, and possibly in financial difficulties. Again, this profile is likely to be shaped by opportunities. This type of staff member is unlikely to be in a position to embezzle funds. However, they may have access to large datasets of customers and clients with personal information, which, in the wrong hands, could be abused.

One of the most salient assessments of this type of fraud still relevant today is Cressey's research from 1950s America which identified the fraud triangle (see Figure 3.1).[15] Fraud occurs when there is a combination of a person with a 'pressure', such as financial worries, gambling addiction etc. combined with a rationalisation, such as a grudge or ethical character that can justify fraud; aligned with an opportunity to commit a fraud, such as weak financial controls. This analysis clearly applies to the 'occasional' and 'fallen' fraudsters we identified; for the committed fraudster it is a way of life and all that is required is the opportunity.

It is worth exploring these three aspects in more depth.

3.2.2 Pressure

There are a wide range of pressures that can cause otherwise law-abiding people to turn to fraud which researchers have found.[16] One of the most common is addiction to alcohol, drugs, sex, or gambling. Such is the impact and cost of their addiction they need to search out for additional means to secure money. Pressures can also be more mundane. The loss of an income in the family, spiralling debts, and marital breakups can all cause financial pressures which, for some people presented with the right opportunity, mean that they crack and commit fraud. Some frauds can be driven by a desire to cover mistakes or malpractice. For example in the case of Nick Leeson, whose fraud destroyed Barings Bank, his initial motivation was to cover mistakes and trade his way out of trouble. Some people who turn to fraud are simply going through a mental breakdown. Some organisations have corrupt cultures and fellow staff may encourage a person to engage in fraud, or they see it as so normal they simply join in (something which will be explored in more depth later in this chapter). In some cases staff are confronted with blackmail or criminal pressures to engage in fraud. Linked to this, some terrorists use fraud as a means to fund operations, and this justifies engaging in it. Finally outright greed is also a common pressure for some to engage in fraud.

3.2.3 Rationalisation

The second aspect of Cressey's fraud triangle is rationalisation. Again, many researchers have identified a variety of rationalisations. Some rationalise their fraud on the basis that their managers and/or organisation treat them badly, so they deserve it. Linked to this amongst many is a perception they are underpaid. Another common reason is that the fraudster perceives 'everyone else' is doing it, so why not me? Other fraudsters perceive – rightly or wrongly – that their organisation is corrupt, and so deserves it. Some fraudsters steal a 'small amount' and perceive that it won't be missed or they will 'pay it back'. That the money was used for a good purpose is another common rationalisation, and this could be a genuine good cause or a deviant one, such as terrorism. Fraudsters also often rationalise their crime on the grounds it won't hurt anyone.

Key Facts

Common pressures which lead to fraud:

Addictions (alcohol, drugs, gambling, sex [prostitutes])
Financial pressures (spiralling debts, loss of income, divorce, etc.)
Covering mistakes/malpractice
Greed
Mental breakdown
Peer-pressure to engage
Criminal threats/blackmail.

Common rationalisations for fraud:

Disgruntled with managers/organisation
Perception underpaid
Everyone else is doing it
The organisation is corrupt and deserves it
It's a small sum which won't be missed
Just borrowing it and will pay back
The money was used for a good purpose
It won't hurt anyone.

3.2.4 Opportunity

It is also very important to stress the importance of opportunity in fraud (as in many other crimes). There is a significant body of research in criminology which links opportunity to crime.[17] Increased opportunities for crime lead to an increased risk of crime. One of the most significant developments in research related to this is Routine Activity Theory, which advocates that crime is likely when there is a motivated offender, a suitable target, and an absence of a capable guardian.[18] Translated to fraud, if a fraudster (either career, occasional, or fallen) is presented with a target (opportunity to commit fraud) and the lack of suitable controls, this presents a significant risk of fraud.

The KPMG research, discussed earlier, found that greed and opportunity accounted for 73 per cent of fraudsters. In 49 per cent of cases the fraudsters had been able to exploit weak internal controls. Further evidence of opportunity in fraud was found by Gill.[19] In interviews with

16 convicted fraudsters of 'large sums' of money ranging from £65,000 to £25 million, it was found that debts, greed, boredom, blackmail, temporary insanity, desire for status, and a corrupt company culture were some of the motivations for fraud. Central to the fraudsters' accounts of how they were able to commit their frauds were weak controls, or, put more bluntly, *opportunities* to commit fraud.

This amounted to the exploitation of systems of checking that only reviewed a small sample of transactions under a specified amount, £750 for example, making it easy to steal sums up to this level. Limited capacity for overseeing transactions was another example, where, in one case, a single accountant and temporary staff oversaw invoices and these were never checked. In one case a fraudster oversaw a £20 million budget and could sign invoices alone up to £25,000 and so he created companies invoicing for non-existent services under this amount. The accounts also revealed the weakness of auditing arrangements in discovering their crimes. It is worth quoting the perspective of one fraudster, Eric, who defrauded several million from his company, on the auditors:

> Accountants can only work on the figures they have got, audit the same. Auditors came to see me and I just lied to them and gave them false pieces of paper and that was that. The checking process was abysmal. I was not worried because I have 20 years' experience of auditors. Had they been better at their job, I would have been in trouble. What I was doing was simple, but the lack of process enabled me to do what I did, the absence of systems, the lack of attention to detail, the lack of knowledge in auditing and accounting. I had three audits in those 18 months ... I gave the auditor the information and he said, 'thank goodness for that', and my thought was, 'you complete muppet' ... There was no interrogation from audit and that was good for me.[20]

It is also interesting to note that most of the offenders did not consider what they were doing to be high-risk or that they were likely to get caught. All 16 interviewees had been caught and this resulted from a variety of sources. Some were caught as a result of external investigations, new members of staff moving to positions of control, new auditors, or anomalies emerging in accounts.

Opportunity is therefore central to fraud occurring. If opportunity can be removed the ability to commit fraud is made more difficult. Situational crime prevention has emerged as a major tool in preventing crime, as it is directed largely at reducing opportunities for crime. These same principles – even more so with fraud because of the large number of occasional and fallen fraudsters – can be applied to fraud to reduce opportunities for the crime to occur. Research on external fraudsters is sparse, as is research on career fraudsters. Nevertheless it is clear that opportunity for these will also be very important, in that they will be actively scanning environments for opportunities to perpetrate fraud. Therefore reducing opportunities to commit fraud is a vital part of the tools used by the counter-fraud professional. This is something which will be addressed in Chapter 6.

3.2.5 Red Flags

Some of the discussion so far can be used to identify red flags. These are indications that there may be a risk of fraud, such as evidence of financial problems, alcohol dependency, changes in mental state, etc. ACFE in their research seek to present statistics on the most significant red flags for fraudsters. In the 2010 report some of the most significant are listed below; these were present in at least 10 per cent of cases:

- Living beyond means 43 per cent
- Financial difficulties 36.4 per cent
- Control issues, unwillingness to share duties 22.6 per cent
- Unusually close relationship with vendor/customer 22.1 per cent
- Wheeler dealer attitude 19.2 per cent
- Divorce/family problems 17.6 per cent
- Irritability,[21] suspiciousness, or defensiveness 14.1 per cent
- Addiction problems 11.9 per cent
- Refusal to take vacations 10.2 per cent.

The most significant red flag was a person living beyond their means. This is an important finding because it is also a relatively easy red flag to notice. If a person is driving an expensive car, wearing luxury clothes, going on exotic holidays, etc. but their salary is only average this may suggest it is worth investigating the person further. They may have won the lottery or inherited some wealth, but they may also be defrauding the organisation. Financial difficulties may also be easy to spot and are simple to pick up through credit checks and searches for bad debts. Some of the other red flags are more open to interpretation and some may be much harder to spot. For example many people with an addiction to alcohol are able to hide this. Nevertheless the above red flags do provide some clues for the vigilant counter-fraud professional to watch out for in those in positions of responsibility within an organisation.

3.3 CULTURES AND FRAUD

Cultures and attitudes to fraud and corruption vary significantly. There are some countries where fraud and corruption are not only tolerated, they are actually admired. Consider the following example: a leader of a country receives a state funeral after a lifetime in office pursuing fraud and corruption. He had been able to amass a fortune of €45 million, or 171 times the total salary payable as a politician, and an official tribunal had confirmed long-term corruption. That leader had stolen €250,000 from a political friend's fund to pay for a liver transplant for his father, and that friend then gave the first reading at the funeral mass! Consider a member of parliament who is found to have received a bribe of €15,000, stands for re-election, and receives their highest ever vote and, in another example, two convicted fraudsters who are elected to parliament. Consider widespread findings of bribery, tax evasion, and fraud amongst the political and economic elite which are rarely prosecuted.[22] The description, you might think, is of a third world country. Many may even be thinking Nigeria. You would be wrong, however, as the description applies to the Republic of Ireland, an industrialised – and most would argue – 'upstanding' country which is a long-standing member of the EU. Juxtapose Ireland to its neighbour, the UK, and the expenses scandal in the UK parliament during 2009. A handful were prosecuted for fraud-related offences and were forced out of office, but dozens more, who had not committed fraud but who had made extravagant but legitimate claims, were also forced out of office. In most of the UK the slightest deviance from ethical behaviour is frowned upon by the electorate and punished.

Different attitudes to fraud and corruption can also be illustrated by some of the several indices which exist relating to bribery and corruption. Transparency International has a number of indices which it publishes, the most notable of which include:[23]

Corruption Perceptions Index: a survey of the perception of corruption in the public sector of countries published annually.

Global Corruption Barometer: a survey of public perceptions of corruption in dozens of countries.

Bribe Payers Index: an assessment of firms' likelihood of having to bribe in different countries.

These all provide useful information for a counter-fraud professional on the likely risks of fraud and corruption in a particular country and, as they are all undertaken on a regular basis, illustrate how cultures and attitudes are changing

It is also important to note that even in some countries where corruption is perceived to be low, there is often evidence of different attitudes to fraud. Many people have views on fraud which consider certain types to be acceptable and this varies from country to country, organisation to organisation, context to context. Fraud often attracts a less ambiguous response: that it is wrong. For example, research in the UK found that 70 per cent of 2,000 people interviewed would commit fraud if they knew they could get away with it.[24] In the UK, research by the Association of British Insurers asked members of the public whether they considered certain behaviours 'acceptable' or 'borderline acceptable'. In these categories 40 per cent rated exaggerating an insurance claim and 29 per cent making up an insurance claim. Conversely using someone else's credit card scored only 6 per cent.[25] In America, research has found that 1 person in 4 thinks it's acceptable to exaggerate an insurance claim and 1 in 10 to add items which were not lost or damaged to their claims.[26] In Australia, 14 per cent of the public have been found to believe that 'padding' an insurance claim is acceptable.[27] Research on expenses fraud found that 34 per cent of Britons thought it was acceptable to exaggerate their expenses in 2007, although this had fallen to 14 per cent by 2009 and 15 per cent admitted doing so (probably due to public revulsion over the expenses scandal of the UK parliament and the recession). When an additional factor – that the company does not reimburse all claims – is added into the equation, 71 per cent thought it was acceptable to exaggerate.[28]

It is also important to consider fraud and corruption at an organisational level. In America, KPMG have published an integrity survey which is based upon responses from over 5,000 people working in a variety of organisations at different levels. In the 2008–9 report they found:[29]

- 74 per cent of respondents had seen or had knowledge of wrongdoing (which covers fraud, discrimination, and anti-competitive practices amongst many others) in their organisation. This compared to 75 per cent in 2005 and 76 per cent in 2000.
- Nearly half had observed wrongdoing which would cause 'a significant loss of public trust' if discovered.
- The main drivers for misconduct were pressures, incentives, inadequate resources, and job uncertainty.

- The sectors with the highest prevalence of 'significant loss of public trust' type wrongdoing were: banking and finance, healthcare, and government and public sector.

The research does highlight some positives over the past three surveys in terms of mechanisms to address this problem (which will be explored in Chapter 6). However, the headline figures across the three surveys over nearly a decade reveal a stubborn level of misconduct observed amongst around three quarters of staff.

A very important piece of criminological research central to many forms of white collar crime is Edwin Sutherland's theory of differential association.[30] In this theory it is advocated that a person's conduct is influenced by the norms of a group(s) they come into contact with. Learning and imitation moulds the behaviour of the person in that group. If in that group the norms are inclined towards deviance, then there is a greater likelihood they will be inclined to act that way, hence 'differential association.' Thus, in a workplace culture, if a new employee is exposed to corrupt and fraudulent practices which are treated as the norm, they are more likely to engage in those forms of behaviour as well. There have also been more detailed accounts of dishonest workplace cultures in practice. Ditton[31] found that workers who perceived they were poorly paid engaged in dishonest schemes to compensate for this and Mars[32] found poor conditions of employment motivated dockworkers to engage in theft and fraud to compensate for this environment. Research by Hollinger and Clarke has linked higher levels of job dissatisfaction and desire to move elsewhere, as well as perceptions of being exploited, with higher risks of staff engaging in negative conduct towards the organisation.[33] Horning[34] has found different levels of acceptability of workplace theft amongst employees, with the theft of small items more acceptable than larger items and with personal property considered definitely off limits! Hollinger and Clarke[35] have also found that the informal rules amongst fellow staff of what actions were acceptable and the sanctions for their breach were more important than the actual rules of the organisation. These informal cultures were therefore considered to be the most important aspect of preventing staff dishonesty.

Another way to look at attitudes to fraud is to consider degrees of honesty. Paul Feldman is an American businessman who set up a company supplying bagels to offices in Washington DC. His model worked on the basis of delivering bagels with a basket for the punters to leave money in, which he would collect at the end of the day. The business therefore rested on the honesty of those taking bagels to pay. In doing business he collected extensive statistics on collection rates, which offers some insight on the honesty of the public. Even in the good offices it was common for 10 per cent not to pay, although theft of the money was very rare at 1 in 7,000. Other interesting trends he found were: small offices were more honest than bigger ones, hotter weather produced higher payment rates, special times of the year such as Christmas, Thanksgiving, and Valentine's Day reduced collection rates. Workplaces with better morale are more honest and the further up the corporate ladder you climb the lower the honesty.[36]

What the above discussion shows is that there is variation in attitudes to honesty and ethical behaviour amongst employees. There will, however, be in almost all organisations a significant minority of the population who will find certain types of fraud and dishonesty acceptable. This will vary according to factors such as the workplace conditions and informal cultures as well as the strategies to deal with it. There is therefore scope to use various strategies to influence the tolerance of dishonesty in an organisation. External contractors and clients can also be targeted with initiatives, but clearly the scope to influence these is weaker. The following discussion will therefore focus upon internal fraud first, followed by external.

Key Facts

Organisational traits which suggest higher risk of fraud

Staff with perception they are poorly paid

Staff with perception they have poor conditions of employment

Staff with high levels of job dissatisfaction

Large number of staff wanting to leave

Tolerance of petty crime/fraud

Immoral/unethical working practices

3.4 CONCLUSION

This chapter has highlighted fraudsters and the culture of fraud. It has profiled different types of fraudsters and shown some of the influences that cause individuals to commit crime. This knowledge is useful and underpins some of the strategies advocated later to prevent and deter fraud. The chapter has also highlighted different attitudes to and cultures surrounding fraud and corruption and has illustrated cues which can be learnt from to help devise strategies to develop an anti-fraud culture, which will be considered later in this book.

FURTHER READING

ACFE (2012) *Report to the Nation on Occupational Fraud and Abuse*. Austin: ACFE.

Gill, M. (2005) *Learning from Fraudsters*. Leicester: Perpetuity Research and Consultancy International.

KPMG (2007) *Profile of a Fraudster 2007 Survey*. London: KPMG.

O'Toole, F. (2009) *Ship of Fools*. London: Faber.

END NOTES

1. Cited in Button, M. (2008) *Doing Security*. Basingstoke: Palgrave, p. 54.
2. See Levi, M. (1981) The Phantom Capitalists: The Organization and Control of Long-Firm Fraud. London: Heinemann; ACFE (2010) *Report to the Nation on Occupational Fraud and Abuse*. Austin: ACFE; Gill, M. (2005) *Learning from Fraudsters*. Leicester: Perpetuity Research and Consultancy International; and KPMG (2007). *Profile of a Fraudster 2007 Survey*. Retrieved 15 August 2008 from http://www.kpmg.co.uk/pubs/ProfileofaFraudsterSurvey(web).pdf.
3. Abagnale and Associates (n.d.) *About Frank Abagnale*. Retrieved 8 August 2011 from http://www.abagnale.com/aboutfrank.htm.
4. Department of Justice (2009). *Sentencing Transcript Dated June 29, 2009*. Retrieved 1 March 2010 from http://www.justice.gov/usao/nys/madoff/20090629 sentencingtranscriptcorrected.pdf.
5. BBC News (2003) *Millionaire's Route to Top Prize*. Retrieved 9 August 2011 from http://news.bbc.co.uk/1/hi/uk/2823407.stm.
6. The Telegraph (2003) *Cheating Major Walks Free Over Insurance Fraud*. Retrieved 8 August 2011 from http://www.telegraph.co.uk/news/uknews/1447382/Cheating-major-walks-free-over-insurance-fraud.html.
7. The Telegraph (2007) *£2 million thief 'lived like footballers wife'*. Retrieved 8 August 2011 from http://www.telegraph.co.uk/news/uknews/1567519/2m-thief-lived-like-a-footballers-wife.html.
8. ACFE (2012) *Report to the Nation*. Austin: ACFE, p. 56.
9. The Times (2009) Accountant at Toys R Us Stole £3.6 million to Treat Prostitutes. Retrieved 8 August 2011 from http://www.timesonline.co.uk/tol/news/uk/crime/article6962406.ece.

10. See Mazar, N., Amir, O. and Ariely, D. (2008) The Dishonesty of Honest People: A Theory of Self-Maintenance. *Journal of Marketing Research*, 45: 633–644; Mazar, N. and Ariely, D. (2006) Dishonesty in Everyday Life and Its Policy Implications. *Journal of Public Policy and Marketing*, 25: 1–21.
11. KPMG (2007) op. cit.
12. ACFE (2010) op. cit.
13. Bussmann, K.D. and Werle, M.M. (2006) Addressing Crime in Companies First Findings from a Global Survey of Economic Crime. *British Journal of Criminology*, 46: 1128–1144.
14. CIFAS (2011) Staff Fraudscape. Retrieved 8 August 2011 from https://www.cifas.org.uk/secure/contentPORT/uploads/documents/reports/2._CIFAS_Staff_Fraudscape_2011.pdf.
15. Cressey, D. (1973). *Other People's Money*. Montclair, NJ: Patterson Smith.
16. Dittenhofer, M.A. (1995) The Behavioural Aspects of Fraud and Embezzlement. *Public Money and Management*, January–March; Cressey, D. (1973) op. cit.; Gill, M. (2005) op. cit.
17. See Mayhew, P., Clarke, R.V.G., Sturman, A. and Hough, J.M. (1976) *Crime as Opportunity.* London: HMSO.
18. Coen, L.E. and Felson, M. (1979) Social Change and Crime Rate Trends: A Routine Activities Approach. *American Sociological Review*, 44: 588–608.
19. Gill, M. (2005) op. cit.
20. Ibid, p. 40.
21. ACFE (2010) op. cit., p. 70.
22. O'Toole, F. (2009) *Ship of Fools*. London: Faber.
23. Transparency International (n.d.) *Surveys and Indices*. Retrieved 8 August 2011 from http://www.transparency.org/policy_research/surveys_indices/about.
24. CIFAS (n.d.) *Employee Fraud*. Retrieved 13 August 2010 from http://www.cifas.org.uk/default.asp?edit_id=579-73.
25. ABI (2003). *What is Dishonest?* Retrieved 26 November 2007 from http://www.abi.org.uk/Media/Releases/2003/02/ABI_Research_shows_insurance_fraud_part_of_public_uncertainty_on_dishonesty1.aspx.
26. Accenture Newsroom (2003) One-Fourth of Americans Say It's Acceptable to Defraud Insurance Companies, Accenture Survey Finds. Retrieved 26 October 2012 from http://newsroom.accenture.com/article_display.cfm?article_id=3970.
27. Baldock, T. (1997) *Insurance Fraud*. Canberra: Australian Institute of Criminology.
28. Vine, D. (2010) Expenses Fraud: A Change of Attitude. In CIFAS, *The Internal Betrayal*. London: CIFAS.
29. KPMG (2009) Integrity Survey 2008–9. Retrieved 5 April 2011 from http://www.kpmg.com/US/en/IssuesAndInsights/ArticlesPublications/Press-Releases/Pages/KPMG-Integrity-Survey-2008-2009.aspx.
30. Sutherland, E.H. and Cressey, D.R. (1947) Minority Group Criminality and Cultural Integration. *Journal of Criminal Law and Criminology*, 37: 498–510.
31. Ditton, J. (1977) *Part-Time Crime: An Ethnography of Fiddling and Pilferage*. London: MacMillan.
32. Mars, G. (1982) Cheats at Work: Anthropology of Workplace Crime. London: Allen & Unwin.

33. Hollinger, R. and Clark, J.P. (1983) *Theft by Employees*. Lexington: Lexington Books; Hollinger, R.C. and Davis, J.L. (2006) Employee Theft and Staff Dishonesty. In Gill, M. (ed.), *The Handbook of Security*. Basingstoke: Palgrave, pp. 203–228.
34. Horning, D.N.M. (1970) Blue Collar Theft: Conceptions of Property, Attitudes Towards Pilfering, and Work Group norms in a Modern Industrial Plant. In Smigel, E.O. and Ross, H.L (eds), *Crimes Against the Bureaucracy*. New York: Van Nostrand Reinhold.
35. Hollinger and Clark (1983) op. cit.
36. Levitt, S.D. and Dubner, S.J. (2005) *Freakonomics: A Rogue Economist Explores the Hidden Side of Everything*. New York: Harper Collins.

4

The Resilience to Fraud

4.1 INTRODUCTION

In this chapter three key areas are considered. The first will be the structures operated by the state to counter fraud, such as the law enforcement community, the system of sanctions and the interest of political elites in fraud. These play a significant part in the overall resilience of a country to fraud. Also important are the strategies of organisations to counter fraud, such as the policy, the assessment of risks, the measures to reduce risks, the preventative measures, the quality of investigation, the sanctions applied, etc. This chapter will examine some of the research on organisational resilience to fraud and highlight some of the weaknesses. Finally it will bring together some of the findings from this and the previous chapters to produce a very early model on the major influences of fraud within an organisation. There is much more research and discussion to refine this further, but the authors argue that with more research and debate it will be possible one day to aspire to economic levels of modelling and predictive analysis within appropriate statistical levels of confidence. At the very least the model offers a basis for strategies to target the major influences of fraud, something which will then be developed in more depth in subsequent chapters.

4.2 NATIONAL RESILIENCE

The state infrastructure focused upon fraud is important in combatting the crime and also, to a varying extent, has an influence upon its level. The most important elements are the investigative resources, the level of prosecution and the sanctions applied to the guilty. Unfortunately in many jurisdictions the state often falls down in these key areas. These will now be considered with evidence from around the world.

It is very common in most countries to have limited resources directed towards the investigation of fraud and those assets are often diluted, with multiple and competing agencies focused upon them. The UK is a very good example of this, with a Government review of fraud[1] noting the following key bodies:

- Serious Fraud Office (270 employees);
- The police (416 police officers in fraud squads);
- Serious and Organised Crime Agency (SOCA) (resource yet to be determined);
- Other Public Sector Bodies: Her Majesty's Revenue and Customs (HMRC) 7,500 staff – including drugs investigators; Department for Work and Pensions (DWP) 3,250; NHS 344; Financial Services Authority (FSA) 46; Department of Trade and Industry (DTI) 150 etc);
- Private sector (in-house investigations departments – the six largest banks alone have 2,500 investigators).

To any map of the counter-fraud infrastructure of the UK must also be added the substantial number of entities in the state, private and voluntary sectors aimed at countering fraud. These might include departments focused upon fraud in companies, local authorities, government departments, charities, etc.[2] Some of these departments may have multiple functions – one of which is counter-fraud – such as compliance, audit, security, etc. The entities countering fraud in the UK therefore range from large statutory bodies, such as the Serious Fraud Office with multi-million pound budgets focused on fraud and corruption alone, to the audit departments of local authorities, which may have one or a handful of staff dedicated to countering fraud.

In the USA the picture is complicated even more by the Federal and state infrastructure. Federal agencies such as the Federal Bureau of Investigation (FBI) have jurisdiction over a wide range of different types of fraud and corruption, such as public sector fraud and corruption, mass marketing fraud and identity fraud.[3] However, there is also the Securities and Exchange Commission, which takes the lead on investment fraud; the Internal Revenue Service Criminal Investigation Division, which deals with tax fraud; the United States Postal Inspectors, mail fraud; the United States Secret Service, credit card fraud/currency fraud; the Federal Trade Commission, consumer and competitive fraud; and many others with particular responsibilities. This is on top of a state bureaucracy of law enforcement which is often as diverse and complex as at the Federal level.[4]

The USA and the UK are typical of many countries with fragmented structures of law enforcement for fraud. This often creates conflicts over cases as well as the ability to avoid some investigations by claiming it is the responsibility of another body. Added to this, many bodies have limited budgets with multiple responsibilities, and it is fraud which is often neglected in favour of what are perceived to be more serious crimes. Consider the statement by a Chief Constable of a UK police force to a bank which had suffered a £100,000 fraud:

> The investigation of fraud is extremely expensive in terms of hours spent obtaining statements and preparing a prosecution case. The Constabulary is required under the Crime and Disorder Act to produce a crime reduction strategy. Our strategy identifies priority areas and police resources are directed to those priority areas. Fraud is not one of them.[5]

Consequently in many countries frauds frequently occur which are reported to law enforcement agencies, but are not investigated.[6] The difference in treatment between fraud and other offences cannot be better illustrated than by the following case. In October 2009 Paul Malina was jailed for eight years after having been found guilty of three cases of attempted robbery and six cases of robbery. He had netted some £17,000 from his raids, which had been perpetrated by handing over a note threatening to shoot the staff if they didn't hand over the money. The police investigation to catch him involved the issuing of CCTV footage to the media and a team of detectives working on the case.[7] However, if Malina had walked into the same banks and attempted to procure monies by impersonating another customer with some of their personal information, it is debatable whether there would have been police interest in even a rudimentary investigation. Indeed, research into victims of fraud found one case of a fraudster impersonating a customer by using a forged passport to empty an account of £9,000 from a bank branch the account holder had never visited; there was no police involvement and limited interest by the bank.[8] Clearly one offence involved the threat of violence and deserved higher priority, but the impact on the bank is still comparable and such a difference exposes the lack of interest of the police.

Indeed one of the striking findings on fraud is the very high attrition rate. Lots of frauds occur but, for a variety of reasons, only a tiny number actually find their way into the criminal justice system and result in a prosecution. Research on the UK based upon data from 2011 found:[9]

Total Frauds	10,133,259	100%
Reported Frauds	157,847	1.5%
Sanctions and Detections	40,709	0.4%

Thus only a very tiny number of frauds result in detection. In the UK if the fraudster is unlucky, he or she will face a criminal prosecution and the case will go to court. If it is a complex case, there is a chance they will be found not guilty by a bewildered jury.[10] If the fraudster is even more unlucky, and is found guilty, the sentence they are likely to face will also be minimal. The Fraud Review[11] commissioned research on sentencing for fraud and this found that the average custodial sentence for an SFO case of at least £1m was three years. The average custodial sentence for fraud in a magistrates' court was three months, which compared to four months for a commercial burglary and three months for theft and handling stolen goods. In the Crown Court the sentence for fraud was 15.4 months, compared to 24.6 months for commercial burglary and 41.1 months for commercial robbery. In America, research on the sentences for a range of Federal offences in 2004 found similar differences. For burglary the median sentence was 24 months' imprisonment and for larceny 18 months. This compared to 12 months for embezzlement and 18 months for fraud.[12]

Overall in America sentences generally are higher, including those for fraud.[13] Consider Bernie Madoff who was convicted of one of the largest frauds ever, amounting to $65 billion in the USA. His punishment was 150 years' imprisonment.[14] He is an example of many white collar criminals in the USA who have faced long terms of imprisonment. Take, for example, Jeff Skilling, former president of Enron, convicted of multiple fraud-related charges, sentenced to 24 years and 4 months and fined $45 million.[15] If Madoff had perpetrated his crimes in the UK he would probably have faced a sentence closer to 10 years at worst, and consequently could have been out in 5 years. To illustrate the point consider the 'British Bernie Madoff', William Godley, who was engaged in a £150 million Ponzi fraud. He was sentenced to only three and a half years in jail.[16] There is also evidence that Americans want even more resources and tougher sentences for fraud and white collar crime.[17]

Aside from social security fraud and expenses fraud by politicians, the media and political elites tend not to be interested in fraud.[18] This lack of interest has significant implications for the resources focused upon it. A popular theory in the criminological literature is the concept of deviancy amplification. This is rooted in ideas concerning the communication of information relating to certain types of crime/deviance. Certain acts of crime/deviance become a focus of attention, which leads to them becoming a higher priority for the law enforcement community, which leads in turn to more prosecutions and convictions, which then reinforces the original focus of attention that the crime is a problem and needs

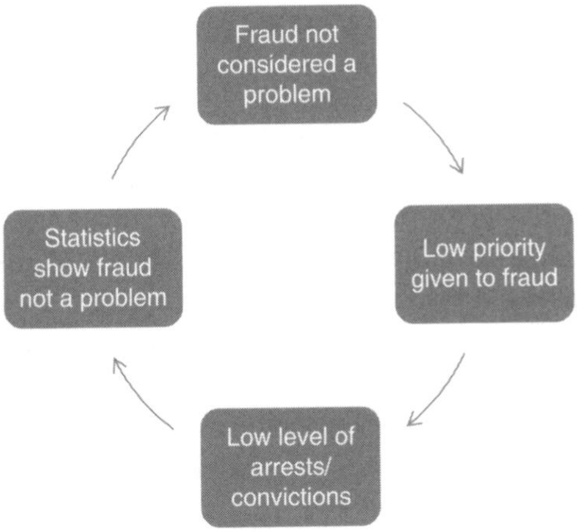

Figure 4.1 Deviancy Attenuation and Fraud

even more attention.[19] With fraud the opposite could be said to occur: deviancy attenuation (see Figure 4.1).

Under this process the opposite is occurring. The political elites in government, parliament and many agencies do not consider fraud as a problem in general. Therefore a low priority is given to it. As a consequence there are low levels of investigations, arrests and convictions. This feeds into crime statistics which do not indicate that it is a problem, and this reinforces the view amongst the political elites that fraud is in fact not a problem, furthering the spiral of declining interest.

It must be noted that there is not a complete neglect of fraud, and many countries are beginning to realise this with new initiatives. In the UK the National Fraud Authority has been created to develop a national strategy to counter fraud and to lead on this, amongst many other functions. Action Fraud has been established to act as a national reporting centre for fraud and to provide advice to victims. The City of London Police has also been made the lead force for the whole country. Nevertheless in the UK and many other countries the following should be noted when considering the state interest in and response to fraud:

- Limited interest of political elites in fraud compared to other crimes.
- Low levels of fraud investigation by state bodies.
- Very low levels of fraud investigation by state bodies of internal fraud within organisations.
- Weak sentences for those convicted of fraud compared to other property crimes.

4.3 ORGANISATIONAL RESILIENCE

With the general absence of a strong state structure to counter fraud, one would have thought that most organisations would seek to fill the gap with their own strong structures and strategies. Unfortunately the research which has been published on the counter-fraud strategies of organisations tends to highlight very variable standards, with far too many bodies having very weak strategies. Some of this evidence will be explored. First, it is important to consider what represent the optimum standards in countering fraud.

The risk of fraud in the public sector in the UK has led to a number of guidance documents setting out model strategies to counter fraud. HM Treasury's *Managing the Risk of Fraud A Guide for Managers*[20] and the joint National Audit Office/HM Treasury *Good Practice in Tackling External Fraud*[21] are examples. Following on from these, and emerging from CIPFA's work on better governance, came the *Red Book* and then *Red Book 2* from the CIPFA Better Governance Forum Counter-Fraud Advisory Panel.[22] This has been produced as a result of the input of various key public sector bodies and experts, and has received the endorsement of the Government's National Fraud Strategic Authority (subsequently the National Fraud Authority) when it was launched in 2008, with the then interim Chief Executive, Sandra Quinn, stating:

> I am pleased to commend the CIPFA *Red Book 2*. This valuable resource provides a holistic framework for countering fraud and corruption that supports and is aligned to the approach of the National Fraud Strategic Authority, which aims to reduce the harm caused by fraud through the creation of a hostile environment for fraudsters.[23]

The authors believe this provides the best benchmark for assessing counter-fraud strategies. It could, nevertheless, be argued that the development of this guidance has been framed with a public sector organisation in mind. However, in the authors' view, the holistic approach outlined in the document provides a standard any organisation – public, private or voluntary – should follow. The standards set out under five sections in the *Red Book 2* are what an organisation should do to counter fraud successfully:

- Adopting the right strategy
- Accurately identifying the risks
- Creating and maintaining a strong structure
- Taking action to tackle the problem
- Defining success.

Table 4.1 Respondents by Sector and Expenditure

	Responses	Per cent	Total Expenditure £billion
Private	26	6.9	114.5
Public	267	71	179.1
Voluntary	83	22.1	3.1
Total	376	100	296.7

The authors have conducted research in the public, private and voluntary sectors on the extent to which they follow this standard.[24] Some of that research will be drawn upon to illustrate the strengths and weaknesses in organisations' counter-fraud strategies. There is also research on the UK as well as other countries which highlights the strengths of counter-fraud strategies. Some of this will now be considered under the *Red Book*'s five key areas. Before doing so, it would be useful to briefly set out the composition of the survey.

The survey of the public, private and voluntary sectors resulted in 376 usable questionnaires, divided between the public, private and charitable sectors as set out in Table 4.1. The response was very good in the public and voluntary sectors, but not as good in the private sector. However, Table 4.1 also reveals that the total revenues the sample accounted for were around £297 billion. If one considers that the GDP of the UK in 2009 was $2,174 billion (World Bank, 2010),[25] which at an exchange rate in 2010 of $1 = 62p, would amount to £1,348 billion, the survey accounted for 22 per cent of GDP. This is a significant sum of expenditure covered. Nevertheless it would be important to note the caveat that private sector responses are all drawn from large FTSE250 public limited companies. SMEs and private sector companies are not covered, and this must be remembered when the discussion on the private sector is considered.

4.3.1 Adopting the Right Strategy

It is important for an organisation to have a clear counter-fraud strategy, with clear objectives and support from the top of the organisation. Evidence from the survey found weaknesses in the private and voluntary sectors, with only three quarters of private and less than half of voluntary sector bodies having a strategy (see Table 4.2). When outcomes and objectives were considered, this fell to just over two thirds in the private sector and just over a quarter in the voluntary sector. There is evidence

Table 4.2 Adopting the Right Strategy

	Yes %	No %
Does the organisation have a written counter-fraud and corruption strategy?		
Public	93.1	6.9
Private	75	25
Voluntary	45.8	54.2
Does the strategy have a clear objective of better outcomes (i.e. reduced losses to fraud) and not just activity (i.e. the number of investigations, prosecutions, etc.)?		
Public	82.9	17.1
Private	69.2	30.8
Voluntary	28	72
Has the strategy been directly agreed by those with executive authority for the organisation?		
Public	91.8	8.2
Private	69.2	30.8
Voluntary	43.4	56.6

in the private and voluntary sectors in the UK of weaknesses in adopting the right strategy. Findings exposing poor practice were revealed by the ACFE *Report to the Nation*, which found that only 39 per cent of respondent organisations had an anti-fraud policy.[26]

4.3.2 Accurately Identifying the Risks

Another important element of a sound counter-fraud strategy is accurately identifying the extent and nature of fraud risks. In all sectors in the UK, there was evidence of the risks being included on a risk register in high numbers. However, when it came to accurately estimating fraud losses, the picture was poor. Less than half the private sector, less than a third of the public sector and less than a fifth of the voluntary sector did so (see Table 4.3).

4.3.3 Creating and Maintaining a Strong Structure

There was a series of questions on maintaining a strong structure, the most salient of which are presented in Table 4.4. They show that using staff who are professionally trained and accredited in counter-fraud is not the norm in the private and voluntary sectors. Only around a third and

Table 4.3 Accurately Identifying the Risks

	Yes	No
Are fraud and corruption risks included in the organisation's Risk Register (or equivalent)?		
Public	75.2	24.8
Private	88.5	11.5
Voluntary	84.3	15.7
Does the organisation seek to estimate the total economic cost of fraud to it?		
Public	29	70.9
Private	30.7	69.2
Voluntary	30.1	69.9
Does the organisation use estimates of losses to make informed judgements about levels of budgetary investment in its work countering fraud and corruption?		
Public	29.8	70.2
Private	46.1	53.8
Voluntary	18	81.9

a fifth respectively had such staff, compared to the public sector where it was over two thirds. Nevertheless the findings illustrate that there are significant numbers of counter-fraud staff who have not received specialist training and accreditation for their role. Another important element of a strategy is for checks to be made on the propriety of new staff, beyond simple references. Here again there were areas of concern

Table 4.4 Creating and Maintaining a Strong Structure

	Yes	No
Have all those working to counter fraud and corruption received the specialist professional training and accreditation for their role?		
Public	69.1	30.8
Private	34.6	65.3
Voluntary	19.5	80.4
Are checks undertaken on the propriety of new staff (beyond simple reference checks)?		
Public	71.4	28.6
Private	57.7	42.3
Voluntary	53	47

with only just over half in the private and voluntary sectors doing this, and just over 70 per cent in the public sector.

Similarly low levels of training were also found by ACFE. In their *Report to the Nation* they found only 41.5 per cent of organisations offering fraud training for managers and only 39.6 per cent for employees.[27]

4.3.4 Taking Action to Tackle the Problem

There were a wide variety of issues explored under the heading of taking action to tackle the problem, and again only the most salient will be considered below. Creating an anti-fraud culture is a very important part of a counter-fraud strategy, but just under half of the voluntary sector and nearly a quarter of the public sector did not have this. The private sector was better in this area, with close to 90 per cent claiming to undertake this work. However, all sectors fell down when evaluating the extent to which an anti-fraud culture was in place, which is clearly also essential. Only around a half of the public and private sector respondents did this and a fifth in the voluntary sector.

Another area where all sectors were weak was in the use of analytical intelligence techniques to examine data and identify potential fraud. Only 60 per cent of the public sector, just under 70 per cent of the private sector and just under a third of the voluntary sector did this. To further deter fraud, it is also important to make use of the full range of sanctions available. In the public sector over 90 per cent had a clear and consistent policy on the application of sanctions, but in the voluntary and private sectors this was just over two thirds. Recovering losses is also an important part of this, and there was evidence of a lack of a clear policy on this issue with 80 per cent of the public sector having a policy, compared to two thirds of the private sector and only 42 per cent of the voluntary sector. Further illustrating this weakness, when asked if they used the criminal and civil law to the full, 84 per cent of the public sector stated that they did, compared to just over 60 per cent in the private and voluntary sectors (see Table 4.5).

4.3.5 Defining Success

It is important to evaluate how well a strategy is working. Having performance indicators or metrics is a vital part of this. There was evidence that this was not happening on a significant scale in all the sectors, with just over half in the public sector, 50 per cent in the private sector

Table 4.5 Taking Action to Tackle the Problem

	Yes	No
Does the organisation have a clear programme of work attempting to create a real anti-fraud and corruption culture?		
Public	77.9	22.1
Private	87.5	12.5
Voluntary	49.4	50.6
Are there arrangements in place to evaluate the extent to which a real anti-fraud and corruption culture exists or is developing throughout the organisation?		
Public	52.3	47.7
Private	58.3	41.7
Voluntary	20.5	79.5
Are analytical intelligence techniques used to examine data and identify potential fraud and corruption?		
Public	60.5	39.5
Private	69.2	30.8
Voluntary	31.7	68.3
Does the organisation have a clear and consistent policy on the application of sanctions where fraud or corruption is proven to be present?		
Public	94.3	5.7
Private	68	32
Voluntary	69.1	30.9
Does the organisation have a clear policy on the recovery of losses incurred to fraud and corruption?		
Public	80.5	19.5
Private	65.4	34.6
Voluntary	42.3	57.7
Does the organisation use the criminal and civil law to the full in recovering losses?		
Public	84.5	15.5
Private	61.5	38.4
Voluntary	63.1	36.8

and less than a quarter in the voluntary sector having such metrics (see Table 4.6).

4.3.6 Overall Analysis

The answers to all the questions in the survey (some of which have been reviewed above) were weighted to allow comparisons across the

Table 4.6 Defining Success

	Yes	No
Does the organisation regularly review the effectiveness of its counter-fraud work against agreed performance indicators?		
Public	56.7	43.4
Private	50	50
Voluntary	23.8	76.3

different sectors. This was done by applying professional judgement derived from many years' specialist experience of undertaking and studying such work. The process is inevitably subjective, but the alternative of not weighting answers is worse and would have ignored the different relative importance of individual aspects of work to counter fraud. The weightings are listed in Appendix 1.

Overall, the most resilient sector was found to be the **public sector** with a mean (average) score of **34.4** and median (middle value) score of 36. The range of scores for those responding ranged from 10 to 45. The **private sector** was next best with a mean score of **30.6** and median score of 32.5. The range was from a low of 6 to a maximum of 45. Worst performing was the **voluntary sector** with a mean of **24.2** and median of 25. The range was from 4 to 41. The standard deviation – which measures the spread of scores around the mean score – again shows the wider variation in performance by the private (10.8) and voluntary sectors (9.2) than the public sector (7.4) (see Table 4.7).

Further sub-analysis of the public sector data was also undertaken and this revealed that NHS bodies were the best with a mean score of 44.4, followed by local authorities with 38.1. Central government departments, agencies and non-departmental public bodies had an average

Table 4.7 Mean and Median Points by Sector

Sector	Number	Mean	Median	Minimum	Maximum	St Dev
Private	26	30.6	32.5	6	45	10.8
Public	267	34.4	36	10	45	7.4
Voluntary	83	24.2	25	4	41	9.2
All	376	31.9	34	4	45	9

score of 36.7 and last were higher education institutions with a score of 28.9.

4.4 FURTHER RESEARCH

Since this survey was undertaken, the authors have obtained further data both from research and from undertaking a series of Fraud Resilience Reviews for specific organisations. The sectors where such work has taken place include the football sector, UK social housing, the hotels sector, and the international mining sector.[28] The results have been interesting. Football, across all leagues, has been found to need:

- a stronger internal audit function;
- more widespread adoption of strategies to counter fraud;
- clearer statements by football clubs of their intention to stop fraud;
- more football clubs having clear plans in place to respond to fraud where it occurs.

Reducing the cost of fraud, as with any business, is an important issue. The financial cost of fraud affects the financial health and stability of football clubs. Regardless of their league, if football clubs want to provide the best deal for their fans, then they need to review current practice and ensure they are properly protected against fraud.

The key findings of the report on the UK social housing sector show that, overall, it achieved a mean score for fraud resilience of 32.3 out of a possible 50. The key findings of the report on the UK hotels sector show that, overall, it achieved a mean score of 25.4 out of a possible 50. This compares with a mean score among public sector companies of 34.4, private sector companies generally of 30.6 and charities of 24.2.

4.5 ACFE RESEARCH

Some of the above research has touched upon some of the ACFE analysis of different organisational strategies to counter fraud. Their analysis provides much more of a focus upon specific measures and their impact upon detected levels of fraud. Such measures form only part of a strategy and there are issues with using detected fraud losses in any analysis. However, their research is useful in providing analysis of the influence of such measures upon fraud. Table 4.8 integrates some of their findings on the prevalence of a specific tool to the media level of detected losses.

Table 4.8 Median Loss Linked to Presence of Anti-Fraud Controls from 2010 Report[29]

Control	Percentage of Cases Implemented	Control in Place	Control Not in Place	Per Cent Reduction
Hotline	48.6	$100,000	$245,000	59.2
Employer Support Programs	44.8	$100,000	$244,000	59
Surprise Audits	28.9	$97,000	$200,000	51.5
Fraud Training for Employees	39.6	$100,000	$200,000	50
Fraud Training for Managers/Execs	41.5	$100,000	$200,000	50
Job Rotation/Mandatory Vacations	14.6	$100,000	$188,000	46.8
Code of Conduct	69.9	$140,000	$262,000	46.6
Anti-Fraud Policy	39	$120,000	$200,000	40
Management Review	53.3	$120,000	$200,000	40
External Audit of ICOFR	59.3	$140,000	$215,000	34.9
Internal Audit/FE Department	66.4	$145,000	$209,000	30.6
Independent Audit Committee	53.2	$140,000	$200,000	30
Management Certification of F/S	58.9	$150,000	$200,000	25
External Audit of F/S	76.1	$150,000	$200,000	25
Rewards for Whistleblowers	7.4	$119,000	$155,000	23.2

The table shows that the most effective control is a hotline. Organisations with this in place suffered a median fraud loss of $100,000 compared to $245,000 for those which did not have it in place. However, despite the difference, less than half of the organisations had such hotlines. Employee support programmes, surprise audits, fraud training for employees and managers were also all influential, producing a reduction in the median level of fraud of 50 per cent or more. External audit of financial statements had the highest prevalence, with 76.1 per cent of organisations having such a measure in place, but the impact was one of the lowest with a median loss of $119,000 for those with, compared to $155,000 for those without. The least effective of all was having rewards for whistleblowers with the median loss for those with this measure at $119,000 and those without it at $155,000; however, the prevalence was also the lowest, at only 7.4 per cent. Nevertheless, all of these measures would seem to have some impact upon median losses. Despite this, there was only one measure being used by over three quarters of organisations, and the top six measures for impact all had a prevalence of less than 50 per cent amongst those surveyed. There are a number of methodological issues which could be identified with the ACFE research, but the data does offer the beginnings of a journey in research to create data on the relative impact on fraud of different measures. This is something we shall return to in the next section in seeking to create a model for assessing fraud.

4.6 UNDERSTANDING THE PROBLEM: FUSING THE FRAUDSTER, THE CULTURE, AND THE STRUCTURES OF RESILIENCE

It seems timely here to bring together some of the findings from this chapter with those of the previous two. From this it is possible to start bringing together a model of the main influences on the level of fraud within an organisation (although many also apply to society more generally). At the heart of the model is the individual fraudster. As was shown in Chapter 3, central to the individual committing fraud is the fraud triangle of opportunity, rationalisation, and pressure. The individual, however, is not in a vacuum, and there is a variety of influences that impact upon them. Chapter 3 also highlighted the importance of organisational and national cultures in influencing whether a person engages in fraud or not. Also important are the strategies to counter fraud at both the national and organisational level.

The model in Figure 4.2 brings all these influences together. The research and knowledge base for fraud and criminology is still not large enough to create an economics type model, where data could be fed into a computer and some of the variables altered to produce different rates of

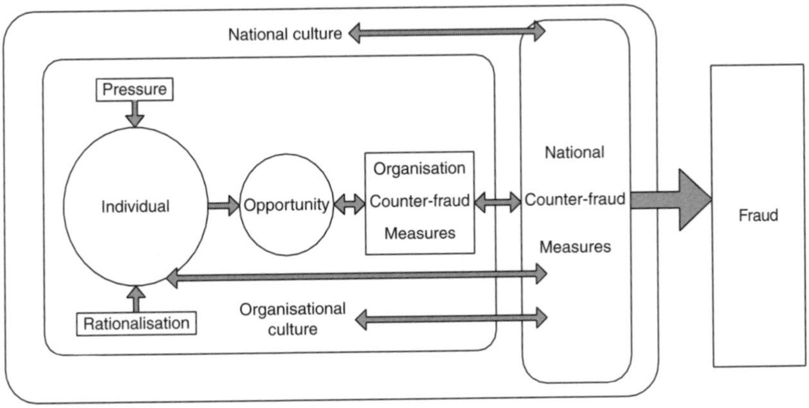

Figure 4.2 The Fraud, Resilience and Culture Model

fraud. We are not in the position to say that, if the organisational culture is changed by x it will produce a y level reduction in fraud. However, we are perhaps at the beginning of that journey. Evidence can be found which shows the influences of different factors upon fraud; we just don't know the exact impact. Thus if opportunities are reduced, so can fraud be. If a person is under financial pressure, they may be more tempted by opportunities to commit fraud. So if the broader financial climate is one of pay cuts, freezes, job losses, etc. there are likely to be more people under pressure, and a greater risk of fraud. If there is a culture where fraud is tolerated rather than a strong anti-fraud culture, there is likely to be more fraud. Organisations with inadequate counter-fraud strategies are more likely to experience higher levels of fraud than comparators with better strategies. If there are weak law enforcement structures, this may mean deterrence is weak.

This very basic model, therefore, provides a starting point for further debate, research, and refinement to produce a more effective approach to countering fraud. It provides the foundations for developing a professional approach to countering fraud, which will be explored in subsequent chapters. Each part of the model provides a place for a multiplicity of actions, which will ultimately reduce the level of fraud that emerges. In the future it may well be possible, to a certain level of statistical confidence, to go to an organisation, undertake analysis of them, then identify a likely fraud rate and apply different actions to assess the impact. This could also be costed, enabling the most cost effective and profitable solution to be created.

4.7 CONCLUSION

This chapter has examined the issue of resilience to fraud. It began by exploring state resilience, largely focusing upon the UK, and showing how there is limited interest amongst political elites, that there is a fragmented investigatory structure with limited resources, and that, in the UK at least, sanctions are also weak. The chapter then went on to examine organisational resilience to fraud. Again, weaknesses were exposed with evidence of significant gaps in counter-fraud strategies in many sectors and in both the UK and the USA. Finally, this chapter drew together some of the findings from this and the previous chapter to illustrate a model identifying the main influences upon levels of fraud within an organisation. The model is very early in its development, but the prospect was held out that, as the research base grows in this field, it will be possible to create more sophisticated models in the future, with a predictive capacity within certain statistical limits. The model also makes clear how some of the influences of fraud can be tackled. These will be examined in the following chapters.

FURTHER READING

Fraud Review Team (2006) *Final Report*. London: The Legal Secretariat to the Law Offices. Retrieved 8 August 2011 from http://www.attorneygeneral.gov.uk/Fraud%20Review/Fraud%20Review%20Final%20Report%20July%202006.pdf.

Gee, J., Button, M. and Cook, I. (2011) *The Resilience to Fraud of UK Plc*. London: PKF.

Smith, G., Button, M., Johnston, L. and Frimpong, K. (2010) *Studying Fraud as White Collar Crime*. Basingstoke: Palgrave.

END NOTES

1. Fraud Review Team (2006). *Final Report*. London: The Legal Secretariat to the Law Offices. Retrieved 8 August 2011 from http://www.attorneygeneral.gov.uk/Fraud%20Review/Fraud%20Review%20Final%20Report%20July%202006.pdf.
2. Button, M., Johnston, L., Frimpong, K. and Smith, G. (2007) New Directions in Policing Fraud: the Emergence of the Counter Fraud Specialist in the United Kingdom. *International Journal of the Sociology of the Law*. 35: 192–208.
3. Federal Bureau of Investigations (n.d.) What We Investigate? Retrieved 11 August 2011 from http://www.fbi.gov/about-us/investigate/what_we_investigate.
4. See Benson, M.L. and Cullen, F.T. (1998) *Combating Corporate Crime Local Prosecutors at Work*. Boston: Northeastern University Press; and Payne, B. (2013) White Collar Crime – The Essentials. Thousand Oaks (CA): Sage.
5. Fraud Review Team (2006b) *Final Report*. Retrieved 28 July 2006 from http://www.aasdni.gov.uk/pubs/FCI/fraudreview_finalreport.pdf, p. 69.
6. Fraud Review Team, op. cit.; Holtfreter, K., Van Slyke, S., Bratton, J. and Gertz, M. (2008) Public Perceptions of White Collar Crime and Punishment. *Journal of Criminal Justice*. 36: 50–60; Calavita, K., Pontell, H. and Tillman, R. (1997) *Big Money Crime: Fraud and Politics in the S and L Crisis*. Irvine: University of California Press.
7. BBC News (2009) 'Threat Note' Bank Robber Jailed. Retrieved 11 December 2009 from http://news.bbc.co.uk/1/hi/england/london/8393374.stm.
8. Button, M., Lewis, C. and Tapley, J. (2009) *A Better Deal for Victims*. London: National Fraud Authority.
9. Button, M., Lewis, C., Shepherd, D., Brooks, G. and Wakefield, A. (2012) *Fraud and Punishment: Enhancing Deterrence Through More Effective Sanctions*. Portsmouth: CCFS.

10. Smith, G., Button, M., Johnston, L. and Frimpong, K. (2010) *Studying Fraud as White Collar Crime*. Basingstoke: Palgrave.
11. Fraud Review, op. cit.
12. Payne, op. cit., p. 369.
13. Fraud Review, op. cit., p. 247.
14. Department of Justice (2009). Sentencing Transcript Dated June 29, 2009. Retrieved 1 March 2010, from http://www.justice.gov/usao/nys/madoff/20090629 sentencingtranscriptcorrected.pdf.
15. Reuters (2011) U.S. appeals court upholds Jeff Skilling conviction. Retrieved 8 August 2011 from http://www.reuters.com/article/2011/04/07/us-enron-skilling-idUSTRE73601Y20110407.
16. Mailonline (2010) Downfall of Britain's Madoff: Smooth-talking fraudster who duped the rich and famous is jailed for £150m Ponzi scheme. Retrieved 18 January 2011 from http://www.dailymail.co.uk/news/article-1300577/Britains-Madoff-William-Godley-jailed-150m-Ponzi-scheme.html.
17. Holtfreter, et al., op. cit.
18. Smith, G., Button, M., Johnston, J. and Frimpong, K., op. cit.
19. Wilkins, L. (1964) *Social Deviance: Social Policy, Action and Research*. London: Tavistock.
20. HM Treasury (2003) *Managing the Risk of Fraud A Guide for Manage*. London: HM Treasury.
21. HM Treasury and National Audit Office (2004) *Good Practice in Tackling External Fraud*, London: National Audit Office and HM Treasury.
22. CIPFA (2008) *Red Book 2*. London: CIPFA.
23. CIPFA (2008) New guide to fight £20bn UK fraud and corruption launched. Retrieved 8 August 2011 from http://www.cipfa.org.uk/press/press_show.cfm?news_id=58967.
24. Gee, J., Button, M. and Cook, I. (2011a) *The Resilience to Fraud of UK Plc*. London: PKF; Gee, J., Button, M. and Cook, I. (2011b) *The Resilience to Fraud of the UK Charity Sector*. London: PKF; Gee, J., Button, M. and Cook, I. (2011c) *The Resilience to Fraud of the UK Public Sector*. London: PKF; Gee, J., Button, M. and Cook, I. (2011d) *The Resilience to Fraud of the UK HEI Sector*. London: PKF.
25. World Bank (2010) Gross Domestic Product 2009. Retrieved 11 November 2010 from http://siteresources.worldbank.org/DATASTATISTICS/Resources/GDP.pdf.
26. ACFE (2010) *Report to the Nation on Occupational Fraud and Abuse*. Austin: ACFE.p. 38.
27. Ibid.
28. Gee, J., Brooks, G. and Button, M. (2011) *Fraud in Football*. London: PKF/CCFS; Gee, J., Button, M., Brooks, G. and Higginbottom, N. (2011) *The Resilience to Fraud of the UK Housing Sector – Research into How Well UK Social Housing Organisations Protect Themselves*. London: PKF/CCFS; Gee, J., Brooks, G. and Button, M. (2012) *Fraud in the International Mining Sector*. London: PKF/CCFS; and Gee, J., Button, M. and Brooks, G. (2012) *The Resilience to Fraud of the UK Hotel Sector*. London: PKF/CCFS.
29. ACFE, op. cit., p. 43.

5

Measuring Fraud Losses and Tailoring the Strategy

5.1 INTRODUCTION

If you don't understand the nature and scale of the problem how can you apply the right solution?

If one went to the doctor with a stomach complaint and the doctor did very little to diagnose the condition and prescribe some treatments, most of us would be disturbed. One would expect a series of tests to accurately diagnose the problem, so the most appropriate treatment could then be applied. One would also expect a follow-up check-up and tests to ensure that the condition was dealt with and the treatment complete. Yet when the problem of fraud is considered in organisations, some don't know they have a problem and others do, but don't know the full extent. Most apply general solutions to counter fraud which are considered to work. It is the equivalent of taking the most popular medicine for a stomach complaint which hasn't been diagnosed. One might be lucky and it works, but there is a risk that it won't, or even worse, that the problem is in fact far more serious. Therefore the authors advocate accurate measurement of fraud as the foundation of any sound counter-fraud strategy. This has benefits not only in identifying the scale of the problem, but also in identifying where the problems lie and in what proportions and, most significantly, it turns the problem into a cost. Once it becomes a cost to an organisation there is much more commitment to reduce it. This chapter therefore explains how it has become possible to accurately measure the nature and scale of fraud, and then to determine an informed strategy to address it. However, before we embark upon this, it is important to consider the far more common premise of developing a strategy based upon risk management and the weaknesses in this type of approach.

5.2 THE PROBLEM WITH RISK MANAGEMENT

The most ubiquitous approach to dealing with fraud is based upon risk management. In this approach a number of key stages to the risk management process are undertaken. First, a process of risk identification is pursued, where the assessor lists a series of potential fraud risks. Second, a process of risk evaluation takes place to determine how likely the risks are to occur, and what the consequences of them will be if they do occur. Third, strategies will then be identified to reduce the risk of them occurring. This could include transferring the risk to someone else (another organisation), avoiding the risk, insurance, and introducing strategies to reduce the risk to – in some cases – nothing.[1] A risk management strategy is better than doing nothing, but there are a number of problems in this process which will now be briefly explored.

The first issue concerns risk identification. Most risk assessments produce lists of risks based upon *past* experience, sometimes in the same organisation, sometimes more generically. They do not take account of new risks which may emerge, so-called 'Black Swans'.[2] Even on past risks, there is much evidence of organisations not learning from the past experience of themselves and others to predict future risks.[3] Expertise is of no benefit either. Research of 27,000 political and economic predictions by Tetlock[4] found that expertise offered no advantage in getting things right. The taxi driver could be just as good as the expert. Relying on a list of potential fraud risks therefore leaves a number of potential risks unidentified, even if you are a counter-fraud specialist with extensive expertise.

The more significant challenge then comes; to evaluate the risks. The first stage – to predict their consequences for the organisation – is less contentious. The much bigger challenge is predicting their likelihood. Frequently this is done in a very basic fashion, using high, medium, and low categories. Often figures are attached to the consequences and likelihood and multiplied together to produce a number. For Wilde,[5] decision-makers vary according to their personality, economic circumstances, culture, etc. and will subconsciously balance risks against potential gains to determine acceptable behaviour. Thus one could give the same risk identification chart to several different counter-fraud specialists and their assessments would all be different.

The next challenge is then the risk management process. Frequently, the person or persons responsible for the exercise will, for risks of a certain score, allocate various forms of controls and strategies which provide a reduction in the risk. A score is created, which invariably reduces the retained score below the 'danger' level. Adams,[6] who has taken Wilde's ideas further, argues that we all have an internal risk thermostat setting our preferred level of risk. For some people the tolerable risks are higher than for others. Thus driving on a road at 100 mph might be too risky for a pensioner, but quite acceptable to a middle-aged salesman who drives extensively. For fraud risks, such approaches are full of subjectivity. Again, different people will rate strategies differently, and to suggest that certain strategies may reduce the risk of a fraud occurring by 30 per cent is often based on nothing more than intuition.

There is also another challenge to the risk management process. Measures to reduce risks may actually lead to increased risk taking. Thus the introduction of the compulsory wearing of seatbelts may have led to some individuals driving even faster than they did previously, because they feel safer in the car.[7] In a fraud context, the introduction of measures to deal with a particular risk may lead to the person responsible 'taking their eye off the ball' because they think they have the risk covered.

One might form the opinion that the authors are completely rejecting the risk management process. This is not entirely true. The authors are advocating the measurement of fraud as the central process of identifying risks. That is, rather than looking at a particular area of an organisation and seeking to effectively guess the types, range, and impact of risks, fraud loss measurement (FLM) is undertaken so as to identify past risks, their impact and extent. There is then much more realism to the risks identified, their likelihood and what their impact will be. There will always be 'Black Swans', but regular FLM and the sharing of the latest trends between counter-fraud professionals can do much to lessen the risk of them. So in short, risk management is better than nothing, but FLM provides a much sounder basis to identify fraud risks, their likelihood and impact. This chapter will now explore how to measure fraud.

5.3 MEASURING FRAUD

Fraud is a challenging problem. Its economic effects are clear: worse public services, less financially stable and profitable companies, diminished levels of disposable income for all of us, and charities deprived of resources needed for charitable purposes. In every sector of every country, fraud has a pernicious impact on the quality of life. However, historically, fraud has been described as 'difficult to cost' and, until relatively recently, it has not been possible to quantify these effects. In the last 10–15 years this situation has changed.

In the UK, from the late 1990s, the Department of Work and Pensions and the NHS started accurately to measure fraud (and error) losses. In 2006, the Government's *Fraud Review* report said, 'better measurement is crucial to a properly designed and effective strategic response to fraud and to supporting better management of fraud risks'.[8] The National Audit Office's 2008 *Guide to Tackling External Fraud*[9] said: 'assessing the scale of loss from fraud is an important first step in developing a strategy for tackling external fraud'. The Government's National Fraud Authority now has a specialist unit devoted to this task, and each year produces an Annual Fraud Indicator. During 2011, the UK Cabinet Office Counter-Fraud Taskforce announced the creation of Counter-Fraud Champion posts in every government department, with a specific role 'to measure fraud and error'. Furthermore, the Secretary of State for Communities and Local Government listed measuring exposure to fraud risk as the first point on a list of things for local authorities to do about fraud.

In Europe, the *European Healthcare Fraud and Corruption Declaration* of 2004, agreed by organisations from 28 countries, called for '[t]he development of a European common standard of risk measurement, with annual statistically valid follow-up exercises to measure progress in reducing losses to fraud and corruption throughout the EU'.[10]

In America, the Improper Payments Information Act of 2002 provided that public agencies should publish a 'statistically valid estimate' of the extent of fraud and error in their programs and activities, and this has recently been reinforced by the Improper Payments Elimination and Recovery Act of 2010. As a result, many more exercises to measure losses have taken place than would otherwise be the case.

The Financial Cost of Fraud Report 2011[11] documents what has been found over the period from 1997 to 2009. It also shows the impact of the recession on losses by comparing and contrasting data from 2008 and 2009 with the prior period. Of course, there are still some estimates published which are simply not reliable. Counting only those losses which are detected or prosecuted, or surveying those working in the area for their opinion, will never be accepted as reliable indicators of the real economic cost of fraud.

Unless one imagines that all fraud can be detected – and research tends to indicate that, at best, organisations can only detect in the region of 1/30th of it – then a measure of fraud based on detected losses will always represent a serious underestimate. Bearing in mind that even the crime of murder doesn't have a 100 per cent detection rate and that the essence of fraud is about concealment, it is unlikely ever to be the case that what is detected will represent the totality of the cost.

Surveys of opinion are also unreliable. The Association of Certified Fraud Examiners (ACFE) in the United States produces an annual survey of this type.[12] Its most recent edition states that 'survey participants estimated that the typical organization loses 5 per cent of its annual revenue to fraud'. Such surveys can represent a reliable reflection of the opinion of those surveyed but, in the absence of an examination of actual items of expenditure and the collation of evidence of correctness, error, and fraud, they are not grounded in fact.

It is now possible to do much better. The financial cost of fraud and error can be accurately measured in the same way as other business costs. This is not unnecessarily costly or difficult, and, most importantly, an accurate, statistically valid figure can be provided for what the financial cost is likely to be.

The volume of data, the total value of the expenditure concerned, the number of different types of expenditure, and the different organisations and countries which have completed such work are impressive. 2011 research reviewed such work undertaken in different countries and across 32 types of expenditure with a total value of £5 trillion sterling equivalent.[13]

It will take a brave Chief Executive or Director of Finance of any organisation to argue that their losses are outside what the research finds to be the case: more than two thirds of the exercises reviewed showed losses (to fraud and error) of more than 3 per cent, with the 12-year average running at 5.7 per cent and average losses rising in the first two years after the start of the recession by over 30 per cent, from 4.6 per cent to over 6.1 per cent. The evidence revealed shows that these losses can be, and have been, reduced by up to 40 per cent within 12 months, and that provides a real opportunity in difficult economic circumstances.

Public expenditure reductions can be less painful if the cost of fraud is reduced; private sector companies can be more financially stable, profitable, and healthy, and the charity sector can increase the resources it has available to deliver on important charitable purposes. Fraud is the last great unreduced business cost, but it can only be treated as such if it is first – like any other business cost – accurately measured. How can this be done?

The first guide to fraud loss measurement was published in 2011.[14] The starting point for fraud loss measurement is a statistically valid, representative sample of payments or cases to be obtained and examined carefully. Central to this is a relatively homogenous group of transactions such as procurement, payroll, etc. (see box below). Consideration is then given to what information is available to indicate the presence of fraud, error, and correctness and what this tells us.

Types of transaction suited to Fraud Loss Measurement

Payroll
Procurement
Housing
Education grant payments etc
Social security payments
Healthcare payments (patients and doctors)
Insurance claims
Tax credit payments
Pensions
Agriculture subsidy payments
Compensation claims

A measurement exercise (for example) concerning expenditure cannot review every single payment which has been made because of the cost and operational disruption which would be involved, so, typically, a sample of all payments or cases is randomly selected. As not all payments are selected, there is therefore some uncertainty in the results from a sample. The sample size is selected to give precise estimates of fraud occurrence calculated on the basis of being able to measure that occurrence to within a given percentage of true value, and with specified statistical confidence levels.

The level of precision concerned varies a little from within 1 per cent levels of accuracy in Europe to within 2.5 per cent in the United States, and with a level of statistical confidence of 95 per cent in Europe sometimes reduced to 90 per cent in the United States. In the United States, the Improper Payments Information Act of 2002 and the Improper Payments Elimination and Recovery Act of 2010 apply, and related guidance determines these minimum levels of accuracy and statistical confidence.

The more accurate the result is to be and the higher the level of required statistical confidence, the larger the sample which it is necessary to examine, and hence the higher the cost. The authors of this book prefer the higher levels of accuracy and statistical confidence as a benchmark for best practice. This is because measurement of the cost of fraud is not simply an academic exercise. Like the assessment of any other business cost, those managing an organisation need to have the most accurate information possible in order to plan, prioritise, and organise its work. If the cost of fraud can be measured and reduced, then this should deliver real financial benefits and resources which can result in higher profits or greater investment in better services or new products. However, if such high degrees of accuracy are not essential this can reduce the size of the sample and therefore the costs of FLM.

The likely level of fraud also affects the sample size. Where fraud losses have not been accurately measured previously, and there is therefore no specific evidence of what losses are in a particular organisation, it is reasonable to assume, as a starting point, that fraud losses will be in the region of 5.7 per cent – the average global extent of fraud revealed by the latest research from 2011.

The higher the occurrence of fraud, the larger the sample size which is required to achieve the same accuracy level. A factor that, by and of itself, does not affect the size of the sample to be examined, is the total number of payments made or cases involved. In fact the sample size can be quite modest, as long as it is representative of the total population.

To meet the standards of accuracy and statistical confidence indicated above, a base sample in the region of 1,800 would be required. However, it is likely that the occurrence of fraud will be unresolved in some cases, because sufficient information might not be available to make a proper judgement as to the presence of correctness, error, and fraud.

In such exercises unresolved cases like this are omitted from the analysis in the interest of statistical rigour, with the results based on resolved cases. However, by omitting the unresolved cases, this lowers the actual sample size on which the results are based.

Therefore, to allow for possible unresolved cases, the sample size is inflated upwards. Best practice would involve an assumed unresolved rate of 20 per cent. Thus our base sample of 1,800 would be inflated to 2,160. The sample size and costs of this exercise might increase if the unresolved rate is higher – or the level of accuracy might be reduced.

The sample is drawn at random from the full list of payments (in the case of fraud loss concerning expenditure) for the period concerned using a series of computer generated random numbers. Because of the variety of costs, more precise estimates of losses to fraud can be achieved by over-sampling the high cost payments and under-sampling the low cost payments.

There are various options to consider for the time period from which the payments are drawn. One option is to sample from a short period of time, such as a recent month. This has the advantage of being current data, but a problem might be that the period sampled could be unrepresentative of the year as a whole. A second option is to draw the sample from a longer period, such as a year. This may give a more representative sample, although if practices have changed over the sampling period, some payments may be regarded as too historical.

Sometimes, it is claimed that fraud loss measurement is too costly to be viable. This is not the case. While ten years ago, it might have taken six people six months to complete such an exercise (600+ days), advances in technology and processes have reduced this to 100–150 days and progress will see these figures reduce further in coming years.

Each fraud loss measurement exercise has a number of stages as can be seen from Figure 5.1 below:

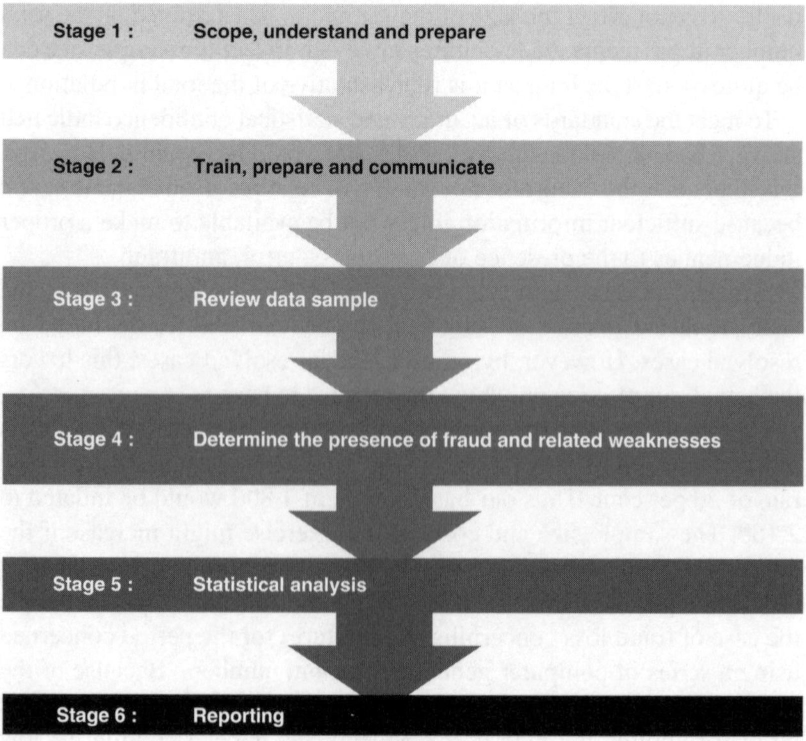

Figure 5.1 Stages of the Fraud Loss Measurement Exercise

The stages are as follows:

STAGE 1: Scope, understand, and prepare

- Identify the data to be sampled and the relevant data fields, and determine the best method of extraction
- Understand the key processes and systems in each area
- Identify the comparator data and information which can be used to help determine the presence of fraud, error, and correctness
- Design and document the exercise-specific procedures
- Design the data sample (by size and nature)
- Review the timeline, resources, and costs.

STAGE 2: Train, prepare, and communicate

- Train relevant staff
- Obtain the data sample
- Ensure access to comparator information
- Communicate the nature and purpose of the work to relevant senior staff, so as to create the optimum client 'ownership'
- Identify potential risks
- Mitigate potential risks.

STAGE 3: Review data sample

- Examine each payment within the data sample
- Collate comparator information (see below) and link to each payment within the sample
- Provisionally group payments according to what the information shows.

STAGE 4: Determine the presence of fraud and related weaknesses

- Determine the presence of fraud, error, and correctness and classify the groups of cases (referred to above)
- Identify the process and system weaknesses which allowed cases of fraud to take place
- Discuss identified process and systems weaknesses with key staff to understand the background
- Supply the processed data, grouped by fraud, error, and correctness, and by value and numbers, for statistical analysis.

STAGE 5: Statistical analysis

- Estimation of the level of fraud by percentage
- Estimation of level of fraud by volume
- Estimation of the level of fraud by financial value.

STAGE 6: Reporting

- Developing, delivering, and explaining a comprehensive report indicating the nature and extent of fraud losses in each area.

The effectiveness of Stages 3 and 4 is very important. The 'comparator information' referred to under Stage 3 is the information which will be used to check the validity of each case or payment within the sample. It is important to consider all information which can reasonably be obtained, which may indicate the presence of correctness, error, or fraud.

To give some examples: in a medical insurance context, is there information which shows that the surgical procedure which has been paid for is impossible? Sadly there is one famous example from the UK where a procedure was supposedly undertaken after a patient had died! In the procurement context, such information might concern the existence of the supplying company, or proof of the actual delivery of the goods or services which have been paid for. In the payroll context, such information might concern the existence of the employee who has been paid (so-called 'ghost' employees are sometimes found – indeed, one example concerned a finance manager who put her entire family on the payroll of the organisation concerned) or whether the employee concerned actually had the qualification or employment history which they claimed to have.

This 'comparator information' needs to relate to two issues. First, has the expenditure been made correctly or incorrectly; and second, if the payment has been made incorrectly, is there any information which would indicate whether it has been made in error or fraudulently (i.e. in the latter case knowing that it was incorrect, or not caring whether it was correct or incorrect, resulting in the receipt of a benefit to which the recipient was not entitled. See the section below on decision-making for more detail.)

Comparator information may be held within the organisation concerned or by an external organisation, and may or may not be in the public domain. This general methodology is adapted into a clear procedure to be followed in respect of each fraud loss measurement exercise in the specific context of the organisation concerned. Final results can then be audited and validated against the exercise-specific procedure. All of the payments or cases within the selected sample are examined – together with their related comparator information – with a view to determining the presence of fraud, error, and correctness.

The first stage of the decision-making is to distinguish payments or cases which are incorrect from those which are correct; the second stage is to distinguish, within the group of incorrect cases, between those which involve merely error and those where fraud is present.

To do this, the accepted civil legal concept of fraud is applied. Why? Firstly, it is important to apply a generally accepted, legally anchored definition of fraud. Some organisations have made the mistake of developing their own definition, but this runs the risk, when applied to fraud loss measurement, of undermining the credibility of the results. Observers might claim that the definition had deliberately been developed to produce measurement figures that showed either high or low levels of losses.

Secondly, it is important that a measurement exercise measures everything that can validly be described as fraud. If one were to apply the criminal definition of fraud (for example in England and Wales under the Fraud Act 2006) this might exclude some losses especially, because of the higher criminal standard of proof beyond reasonable doubt. Fraud can be established (and losses proven and recovered) in civil law on the standard of the balance of probabilities. In any case, the main purpose of the criminal law is to penalise individuals, whereas the main purpose of the civil law is to restore what an individual has lost.

This civil law concept was established in the UK in *Derry v Peek* (1889) and subsequent case law. Internationally, the Swiss Institute of Comparative Law (SICL) examined the basis of *Derry v Peek* for application in 2005. This was set out in Chapter 2, but is worth repeating again here:

> Civil fraud is the use or presentation of false, incorrect or incomplete statements and/or documents, or the nondisclosure of information in violation of a legally enforceable obligation to disclose, having as its effect the misappropriation or wrongful retention of funds or property of others, or their misuse for purposes other than those specified.[15]

It has also been applied in other common law based jurisdictions for the purposes of fraud loss measurement and it is the concept applied in nearly all non-US exercises which have been completed so far.

There are different skill sets which are required to undertake a fraud loss measurement exercise. The authors would strongly recommend that any organisation undertakes at least its first such exercise in collaboration with experienced specialists, who have already undertaken several such exercises, and who understand the issues which need to be addressed to produce accurate and credible results.

These specialists will need to include a suitable, professionally qualified statistician who has previously undertaken work of this specific type to a high standard. The statistician is crucial to both the initial selection of the statistically valid sample, and to the final estimation of the nature and extent of losses based on the findings from examination of that sample. It is also necessary to use professionally qualified fraud specialists (such as ACFS, CFE etc.) who have been trained in this area of work, and who have managed or worked on fraud loss measurement exercises previously.

At the time of writing this book the number of experienced and qualified specialists who have previously undertaken this work is relatively small. However, they are available, and can tackle this work in a cost-effective and timely fashion. Academically accredited fraud loss measurement training is also available. One of the purposes of this book is to spread the extent of this knowledge, and to stimulate wider acquisition of the specialist skills.

The general methodology which has been described above reflects international best practice:

- The methodology was implemented successfully in 11 fraud loss measurement exercises in the UK NHS (the second largest organisation in the world) between 1999 and 2006;
- The Improper Payments Information Act of 2002 in the United States requires public sector agencies to provide estimates 'based on the equivalent of a statistical random sample with a precision requiring a sample of sufficient size to yield an estimate with a 90% confidence interval of plus or minus 2.5%';
- The European Healthcare Fraud and Corruption Network guidance provides for a 'common standard of risk measurement, with annual statistically valid follow up exercises to measure progress in reducing losses to fraud and corruption throughout the EU'; and
- The report of the UK Fraud Review Fraud Loss Measurement Working Group.

The methodology avoids guesstimates, figures derived from detected fraud losses, and figures resulting from surveys of opinion. It reflects a commitment to exercises which:

- have considered a statistically valid sample of income or expenditure;
- have sought and examined information indicating the presence of fraud, error, or correctness in each case within that sample;
- have a measurable level of statistical confidence;
- have a measurable level of accuracy; and
- have been completed and reported, and been externally validated.

The organisations which have already measured and reduced their fraud losses have shown what can be achieved, and have already gained a competitive advantage. Their advantage has been derived from having the necessary information available to them to plot an effective course of action.

5.4 WIDER BENEFITS OF FRAUD MEASUREMENT

The question with which this chapter opened – 'If you don't understand the nature and scale of the problem how can you apply the right solution?' – is simple but telling. There are other questions which require fraud loss measurement to be undertaken, in order for answers to be available:

- How can those leading an organisation know how much to invest in counter-fraud work if they don't know *how much* they are losing?
- How can they know where to invest these resources if they don't know *in what ways* they are incurring losses?
- How can meaningful progress be tracked if there is no information ab*out the cost* of fraud?

Accurate, statistically valid measurement of fraud losses provides the detailed information on which business cases can be written and investment decisions made.

However, fraud loss measurement informs more than just decisions about how much and where to dedicate resources. While there is a comprehensive approach to fraud (described elsewhere in this book) which provides a common framework for action, there is no one-size-fits-all solution. To be successful, strategic solutions need to be designed taking account of organisation-specific information. For example they need to take account of the balance between high volume/low value and low volume/high value fraud, and the impact of different combinations of types of counter-fraud action. These can be tracked, with further questions answered. For example:

- Does it make sense to investigate every example of high volume/low value fraud, or is it more cost-effective to focus on pre-emptive work to change human behaviour (developing a stronger anti-fraud culture and deterrent effect),[16] and to prevent fraud by removing the process and systems weaknesses which provide opportunities?

- If less work is possible (perhaps for policy reasons) to amend processes and systems, will a greater investment in work to change human behaviour compensate?
- If it is possible to address process and systems weaknesses, then how should they be prioritised? The answer to which is, of course, those which result in the largest losses and where there is the greatest advantage to be derived from the smallest investment. Fraud loss measurement provides a statistically valid view of the total *cost* of fraud but also a statistically valid view of the *nature* of the problem. Instances within the sample examined where fraud is found to be present can be 'tracked back' to identify the relative importance (in terms of cost) of particular process and systems weaknesses.
- Where a particular process or systems weakness has become evident as a result of a fraud investigation, how is it possible to know whether this really is important, relative to other such weaknesses?
- How can there be a rational basis for investing in making changes to processes and systems (which are sometimes expensive) unless the related value of fraud is known?

These are only *some* of the questions where answers – provided by fraud loss measurement – can allow an effective strategy to be tailored and a competitive advantage to be gained.

5.5 CONCLUSION

In the second decade of the 21st century, fraud loss measurement and its role in the reduction of fraud costs is one of the few ways for private companies to gain a real competitive advantage, and for public sector organisations to achieve efficiencies painlessly.

This chapter has shown that the foundation of developing a counter-fraud strategy is the measurement of fraud, and has set out the basic principles of conducting a fraud loss measurement exercise. It is to be hoped that this book will further spread the application of the accurate measurement of fraud losses, and the resultant development of effective counter-fraud strategies. Only then will the real scale of losses become apparent, the necessary levels of investment in counter-fraud work be made, effective reductions take place, and the real multiple return on investment be achieved. Resources applied to counter-fraud work should not be considered simply as a cost, made necessary by the requirements of meeting moral and ethical standards; they can and should be an investment in a much greater return, derived from the measurement and reduction of the cost of fraud.

FURTHER READING

Executive Office of the President (2011) *Appendix C. Requirements for the Effective Measurement and Remediation of Improper Payments*. Retrieved 24 July 2012 from http://www.whitehouse.gov/sites/default/files/omb/memoranda/2011/m11-16.pdf.

Gee, J., Button, M. and Bassett, P. (2011) *Fraud Loss Measurement – A Short Guide to the Methodology and Approach*. London: PKF.

END NOTES

1. Button, M. (2008) *Doing Security: Critical Reflections and an Agenda for Change*. Basingstoke: Palgrave.
2. Taleb, N. (2007) *The Black Swan*. New York: Random House.
3. Toft, B. and Reynolds, S. (1997) *Learning from Disasters*. Leicester: Perpetuity Press.
4. Tetlock, P.E. (2005) *Expert Political Judgement. How Good is It? How Can We Know?* Princeton: Princeton University Press.
5. Wilde, G. (1982) The Theory of Risk Homeostasis: Implications for Safety and Health. *Risk Analysis*, 2: 209–225.
6. Adams, J. (1995) *Risk*. London: UCL Press.
7. Wilde, op. cit.
8. Fraud Review Team (2006) *Final Report*. Retrieved 28 July 2006 from http://www.aasdni.gov.uk/pubs/FCI/fraudreview_finalreport.pdf.
9. NAO (n.d.) *Good Practice Guide. Tackling External Fraud*. London: NAO.
10. European Healthcare Fraud and Corruption Network (2004) European Healthcare Fraud and corruption Declaration. Retrieved 12 April 2012 from http://www.ehfcn.org/media/documents/EHFCN-Declaration_EN.pdf.
11. Gee, J., Button, M. and Brooks, G. (2011) *The Financial Cost of Fraud. What the data from around the world shows*. London: PKF/CCFS.
12. ACFE (2010) *Report to the Nation on Occupational Fraud and Abuse*. Austin: ACFE.
13. Gee et al., op. cit.
14. Gee, J., Button, M. and Bassett, P. (2011) *Fraud Loss Measurement – A Short Guide to the Methodology and Approach*. London: PKF.
15. Cited at European Healthcare Fraud and Corruption Network (n.d.) What is Fraud and Corruption? Retrieved 12 April, 2012 from http://www.ehfcn.org/fraud-corruption/.
16. These are separate strands of work which are often confused.

6

Creating an Anti-Fraud Culture and Preventing Fraud

6.1 INTRODUCTION

In the next chapter the costs of investigating fraud will be shown to be very expensive, whether an organisation has the capacity to do so, or it has to hire external expertise. The most cost effective way to deal with fraud is to prevent it happening in the first place. As Chapter 3 illustrated, fraud often occurs because there are opportunities for fraudsters to exploit. Cut off the opportunities and fraud can be prevented. Much can also be done to change attitudes towards fraud and corruption, so that it is not tolerated and employees actively look to participate in the fight against fraud. There are a wide variety of tools which can be used by the counter-fraud professional to prevent fraud. Unfortunately, for many organisations prevention will be viewed as 'financial controls'. These are important, but they are only part of the range of strategies which can be used. There are a variety of measures which can be utilised to create an anti-fraud culture, as there are tools which can be implemented to reduce the opportunities for fraud – so-called situational crime prevention. These strategies will be explored in this chapter.

6.2 SITUATIONAL MEASURES

In Chapter 3 we found that all fraudsters, whether career, occasional or fallen, exploit opportunities to commit frauds. The latter will actively seek them out and may engage in additional conduct to create opportunities as well. Therefore reducing the opportunities to commit fraud is very important. Situational crime prevention is rooted in the importance of opportunity to commit crimes. If environments can be manipulated to reduce opportunities for crime, levels can be reduced. There is a body of research which shows how situational measures can be effective in countering numerous property crimes. Given the even greater importance of opportunity, compared to other crimes, such measures have a major part to play in preventing fraud. Clarke has advocated five categories of prevention: increasing the effort, increasing the risks, reducing the rewards, reducing provocations and reducing excuses.[1] Some of the most salient situational strategies related to fraud will now be explored.

6.2.1 Increasing the Effort

This strategy is based upon measures which make it more difficult for the fraudster to commit their fraud. The rationale is that they will be deterred from doing so or will choose an easier alternative to secure their gains.

(i) Internal controls

For many organisations, internal controls – which are designed to reduce opportunities by increasing the effort – will be the main preventative strategy (some of these also fall under the other category of increasing the risks, which will be explored shortly). Jones[2] outlines a variety of these which are typical of many organisations, with some of most salient below:

Physical measures. Strong-rooms, locks on cabinets, controls on keys, access codes; all designed to make it more difficult for a person to secure access to information or tools which could be used to perpetrate fraud, etc.

Accounting procedures. These include a wide range of reconciliation checks; for example, does the total of salaries paid out match what the staff should actually be paid?

Authorisations. This relates to procedures such as having a person or persons of sufficient seniority to authorise certain transactions.

Supervisory. Are systems overseen by someone to ensure they are being complied with?

Separation of duties. Are different people responsible for functions where, if only one person were responsible, there would be a risk of fraud?

These are all important measures that every organisation should possess and most do (although often frauds occur because the checks such as the above are not followed, rather than not being in place). However, there are a variety of other measures an organisation can pursue to increase the effort for fraudsters.

(ii) Screening

Earlier we illustrated that there are broadly four types of fraudster. For the majority of fraudsters, there is no prior history of dishonesty. This may lead one to the conclusion that there is little point in conducting screening. However, it is important to deter the determined or occasional fraudsters, as the small number that slip through into positions of responsibility can do serious damage to an organisation. Take the case of a Finance Director of a marketing agency who, in 2007, was convicted of defrauding her company of over £2 million in the UK. In her previous job she had been convicted of stealing £25,000 from her employers. She also did not have the qualifications she claimed.[3] This is a clear case where effective screening by the marketing company could have prevented a substantial fraud and damage to their reputation. There is much evidence of prospective employees lying on their applications to increase their chances of employment and to hide past conduct which is likely to end their chances of employment. The Risk Advisory Group regularly publishes research on CVs and their accuracy.[4] In the 2007 study, around 50 per cent of over 3,800 CVs contained inaccuracies, ranging from false qualifications to omitting frauds committed against prior employers. The five most common lies were:

1. Previous positions
2. Employment (gaps, dates, etc.)
3. Academic dates
4. Academic qualifications
5. Undeclared directorships.

An example of lying they uncovered was that of an American national living in the UK who applied for a position in an investment bank. Investigations by the Risk Advisory Group into his application found hundreds of thousands of dollars of bad debts in the USA and a judgement filed against the candidate for $30,000. Someone with such a record of financial management would clearly be a potential risk (for both competence and fraud) for an investment bank. This is why screening is a very important preventative measure against fraud.

There are a variety of different levels of screening and the investment in it should clearly relate to the risk of fraud which the position to be filled represents. Some of the checks which could be applied include the following:

- Confirmation of the identity of the person
- Confirmation of the address of the person

- Credit reference checks
- Bankruptcy search
- Confirmation of employment history, membership of professional bodies and qualifications
- Character references
- Property ownership search
- Legal and judicial data search
- Company directorship search
- Media database search
- Drug/alcohol tests.

For some very senior and important positions further checks may be warranted such as investigations into the lifestyle, family and acquaintances of a person.

Some of the searches above will immediately rule a person out, for instance discovering the person isn't who they say they are. Others will require a risk-based approach depending upon the position applied for and the circumstances, such as a series of bad debts. It is not just employees who should be screened. Contractors working for the organisation and clients with whom business is being conducted may also warrant certain types of screening. Some retailers/financial providers also screen clients/customers before they do business with them. There are providers of services that can check a company, person, card, etc., in a fraction of a second against databases of information. Where there are issues, such as prior fraud associated with a person, address, telephone number, etc., this is flagged up to enable the client organisation to pursue further enquiries to manage the risk. For example CIFAS in the UK holds a staff fraud database, where members who have experienced a staff fraud enter information relating to that case on the database. Employers who are members can access the database to determine if a prospective employee is on that database; if they are, the employer can make a decision on their prospective employment based upon this.

Unfortunately, research suggests that many organisations do not conduct sufficient or effective screening of staff. For example, one study in the UK found that a third of the 350 managers surveyed did not verify applicants' CVs.[5] A study of the UK public sector found little consistency in screening of staff and contractors. There were examples of strategies based upon references only and, in some cases where staff were contracted, it was considered the contractor's responsibility.[6]

(iii) Fraud-proofing

An important aspect of general situational crime prevention is designing buildings and environments to minimise the risk of crime – so called 'secured by design'. There is also a role for design to play in the reduction of the potential for fraud. Fraud-proofing, as it is known, is the process of ensuring that new systems, services, etc. are designed so as to minimise the potential for fraud. It is important that any new service or system has appropriate counter-fraud expertise involved in the development from a very early stage. There will clearly be tensions – as there are in any design-based initiative to reduce crime – over maximising commercial opportunities/making the system or service user friendly versus reducing the potential of fraud to a minimum. The consequences of inadequate fraud-proofing, however, can be dire. For example, in the UK in 1997 a scheme to encourage training through Individual Learning Accounts (ILA) was established, where the Government would provide a £200 subsidy in addition to the trainee's £250 fee. The system resulted in many companies submitting claims for fictitious candidates to claim the £200 subsidy. The scheme collapsed with estimated fraud losses of £110 million.[7] If professional counter-fraud specialists had been involved from the beginning in fraud-proofing this venture, appropriate checks would have been created to reduce the potential for fraud in this scheme.

6.2.2 Increasing the Risks

The second set of situational measures relate to strategies which increase the risk of the fraudster getting caught. Some of the controls listed above can also be identified as measures to increase that risk. Some of the most salient of this type include audits, post-employment screening and testing, independent whistleblowing mechanisms and data-mining/matching.

(i) Audit

In Nick Leeson's account of how his fraud destroyed Barings Bank he describes an audit which occurred when his losses were only £50 million. He describes how the auditors had spent a month in his offices and had failed to discover his fraud. The first draft of their report advocated daily reconciliations of trades. After negotiations this began to be watered down. As Leeson describes, 'When the final report came out, I realised I had got off scot-free.'[8] If that audit had been more thorough, Barings might have survived with a £50 million fraud, rather than disappearing with nearly £900 million. The quote from the fraudster Eric in Chapter 3 also illustrated the importance of audit in preventing (and detecting) fraud. Unfortunately inadequate audit often contributes to and hides fraud. Despite advances in technology, there have been some major corporate failures as a consequence of endemic fraud which auditors have failed to discover. The most spectacular was the collapse of Enron, which prior to its demise had not received unfavourable reports from its auditors. Internal and external audit are therefore very important in preventing fraud. If an employee knows audit is very good and is likely to catch them this may deter them. Central to effective audit is not only employing high quality auditors, but also avoiding familiarity. This can be achieved by periodic changes in internal and external auditors.

(ii) Post-employment Screening

In Chapter 3 some of the pressures which lead to a person committing fraud were identified. These included:

- Addictions (alcohol, drugs, gambling, sex [prostitutes])
- Financial pressures (spiralling debts, loss of income, divorce etc.)
- Cover mistakes/malpractice
- Greed
- Mental breakdown
- Peer pressure to engage
- Criminal threats/blackmail.

Some of these, by their very nature, are difficult to observe. However, some may be observable through conduct and changes in behaviour, such as alcohol or drug addiction. Others, such as financial problems, can be ascertained through credit rating searches. There are a number of cues, or 'red flags' as they are often known, which could warrant further investigations into an employee. Clearly such an approach needs to be risk based. A financial director regularly smelling of alcohol would warrant greater potential scrutiny for the counter-fraud professional than a telesales operative. Also it's important to note that 'red flags', if confirmed, do not mean the person is a fraudster. Many people suffer personal problems without resorting to fraud. Some organisations offer employee assistance programmes for those with such problems to help them to avoid turning to fraud or other deviant action, often with much success in terms of levels of fraud.

There was a famous case of a British Metropolitan Police Deputy Director of Finance who defrauded over £5 million from the police over a period of five years while in charge of a fund for a counter-terrorist unit. This illustrates how post-employment screening could have alerted the police to potential fraud. The Deputy Director had used the money to establish himself as the 'Laird of Tomintoul', funding a lavish lifestyle.[9] Post-employment screening may have established that he was leading a life his salary could not justify, prompting further investigations. It is also interesting to note that screening before he was even given this sensitive post should have raised alarm bells, as he had previously 'mistakenly' paid several thousand pounds destined for the police welfare fund into his own bank account.[10]

Some organisations also conduct tests on employees in certain positions on an ongoing basis, such as drug/alcohol tests as well as integrity tests. There are important issues of balancing a person's privacy against reasonable intrusions, to ensure that the risk of fraud, amongst many other potential risks, is balanced. In the UK, research by the Joseph Rowntree Foundation[11] has suggested that drug testing does not warrant the intrusion in privacy, given its effectiveness, and that there are more robust measures to identify and deal with this problem. In the USA, however, such tests are used by many organisations. Clearly there are legal challenges to conducting such tests, depending upon the jurisdiction.

Perhaps a more effective approach is to encourage managers to look for 'red flags' which may indicate a person is at higher risk of committing fraud, triggering further investigations. CIFAS (n.d.) identify a number of potential cues/red flags:

- Staff under stress without a high workload – marked personality changes
- Always working late
- Reluctance to take leave
- Unexplained wealth or living beyond apparent means
- Sudden change of lifestyle
- Customer complaints of missing statements, unrecognised transactions
- New staff resigning quickly
- Cosy relationships with suppliers/contractors
- Suppliers/contractors who insist on dealing with just one individual
- Rising costs with no explanation

- Key employees having too much control or authority without audit checks
- Employees with external business interests.

(iii) Tests

Integrity tests are closely associated with programmes to root out corrupt police officers. Integrity tests – where specialists impersonate staff, customers or the public – to ascertain inappropriate behaviour also have a role to play in a counter-fraud preventative strategy.[12] The Government Accountability Office (GAO) in the USA regularly uses tests and publishes the results to expose the standards of bodies in countering fraud. Sometimes they expose outright corruption. For example, in one investigation of For-Profit Colleges who receive Federal funding, staff impersonated students and applied to 15 colleges. The GAO found four colleges encouraging students to engage in fraudulent practices and all of them made deceptive or questionable statements. As an example of the former, one college asked an applicant to remove $250,000 of savings from his statement so he would be eligible for Federal funds.[13] The GAO in other tests has been more focused upon the robustness of counter-fraud systems. For example, in another operation the GAO applied for seven US passports using false information and documents produced from software easily available in the high street. They managed to receive three passports, two were also issued, but later recovered in the post and only two were denied.[14]

(iv) Hotlines

There are many employees in an organisation who identify malpractice or have suspicions but are reluctant to put their 'head over the parapet' for fear of the consequences to their position. The person they report it to may be involved in the malpractice, or it may be proved wrong leading to consequences for their career. One way around this is for organisations to set up whistleblowing mechanisms where a person can phone a dedicated hotline/go to a webpage and report their concerns anonymously. Ideally this should be overseen by a separate department and an even more effective strategy is to have another organisation take responsibility. Then there are clear dividing lines and the whistleblower can be certain that their concern will be taken seriously. Such measures also encourage more staff to report malpractice because there is less risk they will be identified and revenge inflicted upon them. Independent whistleblowing schemes are therefore an important part of increasing surveillance. A fraudster – even if colluding with managers – will know that any person with suspicions can navigate around them to report, and, if taken seriously, it will be harder for them to frustrate any investigation. Indeed research by ACFE has found anonymous reporting lines as the most successful mechanism for detecting fraud. ACFE also found that those organisations with hotlines generally lost less money to fraud. The median loss for an organisation with a hotline was $100,000 and without, $245,000, a 59.2 per cent reduction, the highest of all measures assessed by ACFE.[15]

(v) Data-sharing, matching and mining

In a number of sectors, counter-fraud professionals have come together in various forums to share intelligence on fraudsters and their latest techniques. There are also a variety of data-mining and matching strategies that can be pursued, which act as a means of discouraging fraudsters because of the surveillance function they provide, but they also provide the basis for pro-active investigative techniques. As these are central to a pro-active investigative function, all of these will be explored in more depth in the next chapter on the investigation and detection of fraud.

6.2.3 Reducing Rewards

Reducing rewards encompasses a number of strategies which are best dealt with in Chapter 8. The most significant of these are legal measures to seek redress from fraudsters so they lose any gains they have made from their crimes. There are also some preventative measures which can be used. One of the most common controls that fits this category is reducing to a minimum the authorisation level for expenditures which require only one person to authorise them. For example, if a person responsible for paying invoices can only authorise up to x amount without needing an additional authoriser, that restricts their potential gains to the region of x.

6.2.4 Reducing Provocations and Excuses

The final categories Clarke advocated were reducing provocations and excuses. These are heavily linked to developing an anti-fraud culture, which will be discussed shortly; therefore, the measures which fall under this will be considered under that category.

6.2.5 Displacement

It is important to consider the fundamental weakness of situational crime prevention: displacement. A variety of displacements have been identified by researchers;[16]

- *Temporal.* The crime is committed at a different time.
- *Tactical.* The crime is committed using a different method.
- *Target.* The crime is committed against a different target.
- *Territorial.* The crime is committed in a different area.
- *Functional.* A different type of crime is committed.
- *Perpetrator displacement.* Prevented crimes are committed by different offenders.

Many fraudsters fall into the categories of the fallen and occasional as discussed above. For these it is unlikely if the opportunity is removed that they will move to another target, use a different method or switch to armed robbery etc. Except for the most determined fraudsters, displacement is unlikely to be as significant as for other volume crimes. This demonstrates the huge potential of situational measures.

6.3 CREATING AN ANTI-FRAUD CULTURE

In Chapter 3 corrupt and fraudulent cultures were explored. It was shown that there are both organisational and national cultures which differ in attitudes towards honesty, fraud and corruption etc. Such cultures can be changed and the following section will reveal some of the strategies which can be pursued to do this.

6.3.1 A Model Anti-Fraud Culture Strategy

The first part of any anti-fraud culture strategy is the publication of a clear statement on the expectations of behaviour of an employee/contractor etc. Those engaged in dishonest behaviour will often state they did not know they were breaking any rules. Therefore statements of expectations of behaviour and the potential sanctions for breach are very important. All those concerned should be issued with the statement and, ideally, should be informed about them in fraud awareness training. This should also clearly set out the procedures for dealing with fraud and corruption. The importance of this type of approach has been illustrated by research on dishonesty. In psychological tests to determine levels of dishonesty, it was found that exposure to the Ten Commandments before a test significantly reduced the level of cheating.[17]

This is the next important aspect of a counter-fraud strategy – fraud awareness training. Again, there is mixed evidence of the use of such measures. In a survey of the UK central Government, less than half the organisations indicated that they had such measures and those that said they did were often stretching the point, with measures implemented only for induction of new employees, by computer training package or via the notice board.[18] To be more effective, fraud awareness training should be more extensive than this. Regular training for *all* staff, newsletters, e-mails and fraud awareness periods should all be used to mobilise the honest majority. Such training should cover:

- Types of frauds and scams
- Expectations of behaviour
- Examples of fraudulent behaviour
- The damage fraud does to an organisation
- What happens to those detected defrauding
- How to report fraud.

Frequently, frauds occur because procedures are not followed properly. Staff are not properly supervised, authorisations which are supposed to happen are overridden, separate duties become merged – to name a few. It is important that the training also highlights to staff the importance of following procedures correctly and not deviating from them.

Publicity is very important. Some organisations bring to light cases of fraudsters who have been caught and highlight the sanctions that have been applied. Some list their activities to show how active they are in dealing with fraud. They also highlight the damage fraud has done to the organisation, as well as how to report fraud if it is suspected. Some organisations publicise the latest scams that staff need to be aware of. These are all important elements of raising the profile of the issue to enhance the anti-fraud culture of the organisation.

More generally with regard to tackling crime, Bowers and Johnson[19] have identified a wide range of publicity tools that can be used to prevent deviance from offender-targeted strategies, such as personal communications with known offenders; strategies to encourage public action, such as crime prevention advice; to increase crime prevention intervention publicity, such as release of information to the media about success or an impending crackdown. Indeed, Laycock[20] has found evidence of how intense local and national press coverage of an initiative led to a reduction in the rate of burglary.

The discussion above also highlights the importance of the workplace culture in influencing levels of dishonesty. Enhancing the pay and conditions of staff and levels of job satisfaction would have benefits in reducing the risk of fraud in an organisation. However, these issues are beyond the competence of a counter-fraud specialist to change. They could, nevertheless, bring these issues to the attention of key decision-makers, so they are aware that the consequences of the conditions of the organisation have implications for fraud and other related risks. Strategies to improve these may have wider benefits to the body.

> The English Counter Fraud Service of the National Health Service (known as NHS Protect) provides a model strategy for developing a counter-fraud culture. Some of the initiatives include:
>
> Delivering fraud awareness training to NHS staff and key agencies
> Developing relationships with key-decision-makers and signing agreements with key professional bodies relating to countering fraud
> Publishing a quarterly magazine focused upon fraud to strengthen the anti-fraud culture
> Obtaining media coverage on fraud cases and their outcomes
> Running awareness campaigns such as a fraud awareness month
> Giving resources to counter-fraud specialists to conduct anti-fraud campaigns.[21]

Many of the measures described above are relatively easy to implement within an organisation. However, fraud comes from external sources as well and here efforts to create an anti-fraud culture pose more challenges, as there is not a 'captive' audience with sanctions which can be applied for non-compliance. One example that has had some success is the UK Department for Work and Pensions, which has responsibility for administering social security payments and has conducted a campaign to change the public's attitude to welfare fraud. This has included television advertisements highlighting the strategies being used to catch fraudsters, as well as what happens if you are caught. Posters were also used, including mock posters offering cash-in-hand work, as well as advertisements on buses and in local newspapers. Between 2005–6, independent research conducted found there was an increase from 75 per cent to 83 per cent of the public who strongly agree it is wrong to claim benefits to which you are not entitled.[22]

6.3.2 Deterrence

It is worth focusing upon the importance of deterrence in creating an anti-fraud culture. Deterrence is an important part of any preventative strategy. Hollinger and Davis[23] have argued that '[p]erhaps the single most important factor influencing employees' decisions to steal involves whether they will get caught or not'. Linked to this is the penalty the fraudster receives for their crime. If – as is common – the fraudster is not prosecuted, or if prosecuted is convicted and only gets a light sentence, this does not send out a message that the consequences for engaging in fraud will be dire.[24] In the USA many public and private bodies actively engage in parallel proceedings using criminal, civil, regulatory and administrative sanctions.[25] In the UK this is rarer, but in the NHS a policy of 'parallel sanctions' is often pursued, as well as publicised. This involves a combination of criminal prosecution, disciplinary procedures and – where a licence to practice is involved – attempting to have the fraudster struck off. In addition to this, the NHS will also pursue a civil action to recoup its losses. To illustrate the case, in 2006 a dentist was struck off by the General Dental Council after being convicted of defrauding the NHS of almost £200,000. In a prior action he had been jailed for 18 months. Action was also pursued to recover the monies lost.[26] This will be considered further in Chapter 8.

6.3.3 Reputation

Wilson and Kelling[27] have famously argued that broken windows lead to more broken windows. This has spawned a multiplicity of strategies that seek to enhance security via dealing with these trivial acts – so called zero tolerance policing. These same signals of social decay, we argue, can be applied to countering fraud in what could be described as 'broken ethics', which, if not properly dealt with, are likely to lead to further 'broken ethics'. If an organisation begins to fail to address trivial acts of dishonesty, the authors believe that this can create a culture where such acts of dishonesty become increasingly acceptable. Skogan[28] – writing about the same broken windows – has described this as 'spirals of decay'. It is therefore very important in an organisation to deal with all of the most basic transgressions of rules regarding acceptable behaviour, before it spirals into a 'broken, corrupt culture'.

Linked to ensuring that 'broken ethics' are dealt with is the importance of the reputation of the counter-fraud infrastructure. A reputation for incompetence and the perception that there will be little interest in 'minor transgressions' is likely to encourage some potential fraudsters. Button[29] has illustrated how the reputation of a security department is important in deterring certain criminal activities. He cites the example of El Al security, where, despite the desire of many terrorist groups to attack the airline, it has very rarely been targeted, let alone successfully attacked. Such is the reputation for the quality of their security that terrorist groups would be unlikely to consider targeting them. This same reputation is important in countering fraud. Securing a reputation for detecting fraud quickly, investigating it effectively and securing sanctions sends out a message to potential fraudsters, that engaging in dishonest practices in this body poses a higher risk.

In essence, this is building upon the work of Eco[30] regarding signals and the disproportionate effect that certain events have upon a person's perception of risk. Therefore if a counter-fraud specialist can pursue a strategy which sends out a clear message that fraud will be detected and dealt with, and that the consequences will be severe, this may disproportionately affect fraudsters' perception of how risky their deviant venture might be.

6.4 CONCLUSION

This chapter has considered the measures an organisation can pursue in order to prevent fraud and develop an anti-fraud culture. It has shown that there are a very wide range of measures that can be pursued, which go beyond traditional accounting controls. Potential employees, contractors and clients can be screened to assess their potential risk of fraud. New services and products – as well as existing ones – can be fraud-proofed to minimise the risk of fraud. Audits can be made more effective to deter and detect fraudsters. Tests can be undertaken to root out fraudulent activities and unethical behaviour. Data can be shared, matched and mined to deter and detect fraudsters. A variety of measures can also be pursued to develop an anti-fraud culture. Setting clear statements of ethical behaviour, fraud awareness training can be provided and campaigns used. Finally, the organisation can do much to create a model workplace where many of the traits which breed fraud and corruption are removed. The box below brings all these strategies together to illustrate a model anti-fraud culture and prevention strategy.

Model Anti-Fraud Culture and Prevention Strategy

Controls
Screening
Fraud-proofing
Effective audit
Tests
Hotlines
Data-sharing, matching and mining
Statements of ethical behaviour
Fraud awareness training
Publicity campaigns
Maximising reputation
Creating the model workplace

FURTHER READING

ACFE (n.d.) *Fraud Prevention Check Up*. Available at http://www.acfe.com/resources/publications.asp?copy=fraudprevention.

CIFAS and Chartered Institute of Personnel and Development (n.d.) *Tackling Staff Fraud and Dishonesty: Managing and Mitigating the Risks*. Available at http://www.cifas.org.uk/secure/contentPORT/uploads/documents/Staff%20 Fraud/CIPDGuide.pdf.

Fraud Advisory Panel (n.d.) Fighting Fraud a Guide for SMEs. Available at http://www.fraudadvisorypanel.org/newsite/PDFs/advice/FightingFraud 2ndEdition.pdf.

National Audit Office (n.d.) *Fraud Prevention Guidance*. Available at http://www.nao.org.uk/guidance_and_good_practice/good_practice/fraud_and_corruption.aspx.

END NOTES

1. Clarke, R.V.G. (2005) Seven Misconceptions of Situational Crime Prevention. In, Tilley, N. (ed), *Handbook of Crime Prevention and Community Safety*. Cullompton: Willan.

2. Jones, P. (2004) *Fraud and Corruption in Public Services*. Aldershot: Gower.
3. Edwards, R. (2007) *£2m Thief 'Lived Like a Footballer's Wife'*. Retrieved 15 January 2008, from *Daily Telegraph* website.
4. Risk Advisory Group (2008) Press Release. Retrieved 8 August 2010 from http://www.riskadvisory.net/news/82/81/.
5. BBC News (2001) *One in Three 'Lie on CVs'*. Retrieved 18 October 2007 from http://news.bbc.co.uk/1/hi/business/1475221.stm.
6. Button, M. and Brooks, G. (2009) 'Mind the Gap', Progress Towards Developing Anti-fraud Culture Strategies in UK Central Government Bodies. *Journal of Financial Crime*, 16: 229–244.
7. Doig, A. (2007) *Fraud*. Cullompton: Willan.
8. Leeson, N. (1996) *Rogue Trader*. London: Little Brown, p. 90.
9. Jones, P. (2004). *Fraud and Corruption in Public Services*. Aldershot: Gower.
10. Tickner, P (2010) *How to be a Successful Frauditor*. Chichester: John Wiley & Sons.
11. Joseph Rowntree Foundation (2004) *Drug Testing at Work: Summary Conclusions of the Independent Inquiry into Drug Testing at Work*. Retrieved 12 August 2011 from http://www.jrf.org.uk/publications/drug-testing-workplacesummary-conclusions-independent-inquiry-drug-testing-work.
12. Button, M. (2008) *Doing Security: Critical Reflections and an Agenda for Change*. Basingstoke: Palgrave.
13. GAO (2010a) *For Profit Colleges Undercover Testing Finds Colleges Encouraged Fraud and Engaged in Deceptive and Questionable Marketing Practices*. Retrieved 12 August 2011 from http://www.gao.gov/new.items/d10948t.pdf.
14. GAO (2010b) *State Department Undercover Tests Show Passport Issuance Process Remains Vulnerable to Fraud*. Retrieved 12 August 2011 from http://www.gao.gov/new.items/d10922t.pdf.
15. ACFE (2010) *Report to the Nation on Occupational Fraud and Abuse*. Austin: ACFE, p. 43.
16. Barr, R. and Pease, K. (1990). Crime Placement, Displacement and Deflection. In Tonry, M. and Morris, N. (eds), *Crime and Justice: A Review of Research*. Chicago: University of Chicago Press, pp. 277–318; Reppetto, T. (1976) Crime Prevention and the Displacement Phenomenon. *Crime and Delinquency*, 22: 166–177.
17. See Mazar, N., Amir, O. and Ariely, D. (2008) The Dishonesty of Honest People: A Theory of Self-Maintenance. *Journal of Marketing Research*, 45: 633–644; Mazar, N. and Ariely, D. (2006) Dishonesty in Everyday Life and Its Policy Implications. *Journal of Public Policy and Marketing*, 25: 1–21.
18. Button and Brooks, op. cit.
19. Bowers, K. and Johnson, S. (2005) Using Publicity for Preventative Purposes. In, Tilley, N. (ed), *Handbook of Crime Prevention and Community Safety*. Cullompton: Willan.
20. Laycock, G. (1991) Operation Identification or the Power of Publicity. *Security Journal*, 2: 67–71.
21. NAO (n.d.) *Good Practice Guide. Tackling External Fraud*. London: NAO.
22. NAO, op. cit.
23. Hollinger, R.C. and Davis, J.L. (2006) Employee Theft and Staff Dishonesty. In Gill, M. (ed.) *The Handbook of Security*. Basingstoke: Palgrave, pp. 203–228, at p. 218.

24. Levi, M. (2006) *Sentencing Frauds: A Review*. Retrieved 28 May 2009 from http://www.cf.ac.uk/socsi/resources/Levi_GFR_Sentencing_Fraud.pdf; Fraud Review Team (2006b) *Final Report*. Retrieved 28 July 2006 from http://www.aasdni.gov.uk/pubs/FCI/fraudreview_finalreport.pdf.
25. Payne, B. (2013) *White Collar Crime – The Essentials*. Thousand Oaks (CA): Sage, chapter 13.
26. BBC News (2006a). *Dentist Struck Off for NHS Fraud*. Retrieved 18 October 2007 from http://news.bbc.co.uk/1/hi/england/london/5181706.stm.
27. Wilson, J.Q. and Kelling, G.L. (1982) Broken Windows: The Police and Neighbourhood Safety. *The Atlantic Monthly*, (March): 29–38.
28. Skogan, W. (1990) *Disorder and Decline: Crime and the Spiral of Decay in American Neighbourhoods*. New York: Free Press.
29. Button (2008) op. cit.
30. Eco, U. (1976) *A Theory of Semiotics*. Bloomington: Indianapolis University Press.

7

Detecting Fraud and Investigating Professionally

7.1 INTRODUCTION

In this chapter we explore the detection and investigation of fraud. We start by illustrating the costs of fraud investigation, because it is expensive, and highlight further the importance of preventative measures discussed earlier. After doing this, we examine who investigates fraud. The chapter then moves on to consider the importance of proactive investigation and some of the strategies which can be used, as well as making reactive investigations more effective. The main elements of conducting fraud investigations are then explored, highlighting best practice from the literature. The chapter ends with a consideration of what psychology can offer the investigator in enhancing their skills, particularly in detecting deception.

7.2 THE COSTS OF INVESTIGATION

Estimating the costs of any type of criminal investigation is fraught with difficulty. For example, in the UK there has been much interest in the media directed at the cost of investigating alleged frauds by Members of Parliament relating to their expense claims. In one such example in March 2010, the British newspaper, *The Guardian*, ran a story stating that, since the outbreak of the scandal in May 2009, the costs of the 13 police officers investigating the fraud had amounted to over £500,000.[1] This largely related to the salaries of the officers. However, one could argue that those officers would have been paid anyway and the real cost should be additional costs: over-time required, and the opportunity cost of the other frauds/crimes they could have been investigating. At an organisational level, however, one could focus the costs of investigation on the salaries and resources of those involved in investigating fraud and/or any additional costs related to external help in an investigation. In the latter, it is possible to give a clearer indication of costs. Whichever method is used, however, fraud investigation is expensive.

If a medium-sized organisation experienced a fraud of £100,000 of average complexity and, because of the lack of an internal resource, they sought the help of a firm of professional investigators such as KPMG, PwC, PKF etc., they could expect to pay in the region of £30,000 for the fraud to be investigated. If the investigation were more complex and involved an international dimension this figure could be much higher. An organisation could thus suffer a £100,000 fraud, pay £30,000 to have it investigated and might not even secure the return of any of the monies, thus adding to the cost impact of the fraud. Some frauds amount to very large sums of money and attract equally large costs of investigation. The authors are aware of one fraud involving a major financial institution which amounted to £50 million. This was investigated by a large professional services firm at a cost of about £13 million; the investigation identified the culprits, but, to save the reputation of the financial institution, did not result in any legal action.

Fraud investigation is, therefore, not a cheap option, and it is much better to invest resources to minimise the occurrence of fraud. The first reaction of a senior manager, and even some fraud specialists, to some frauds is that the actual costs of the investigation set against what might be returned on a pure cost–benefit analysis, mean that it is not worth investing in the investigation. It is important, nevertheless, as part of the overall counter-fraud strategy, to investigate frauds when they do occur as part of the development of an anti-fraud culture. Not investigating could send out a message that fraud is not taken seriously and that it is worth the risk of perpetrating fraud.

7.3 WHO WILL INVESTIGATE?

In Chapter 4 the fragmented state law enforcement entities which are focused upon fraud, combined with often limited resources and the prioritisation of other crimes, were highlighted. It is no surprise to find that a fraud of a significant sum of money could occur against an organisation and that there is prima facie evidence of who has committed it, but when the police or other public law enforcement bodies are called, they decline, or are unable, to investigate it. This is very common in the UK as well as many other countries.[2] If an organisation does want police involvement (and many won't), what is usually required is the production of all the evidence such that it would be ready to prosecute. This means that most organisations have to investigate fraud themselves or turn to an external body with expertise. As shown earlier this can be expensive.

7.3.1 Investigative Resources

Many SMEs will not have the capacity to have their own fraud investigative resource. Any initial investigations are likely to be undertaken by an auditor, accountant, general manager or HR manager, to name the most common. These are unlikely to have training that equips them to investigate to a standard where criminal prosecution is possible. For many of these bodies, in the absence of police involvement they will invariably have to turn to external expertise in the form of an accountancy or private investigation firm. There are many challenges to hiring the best, which we will return to later. The costs of doing this can be expensive and so for many SMEs, unless the cost of fraud is substantial, there may be a reluctance to pursue the matter any further.

In larger organisations there tends to be a number of specialist occupations which become involved in investigating fraud. The most common are auditors who have responsibility for verifying the validity and accuracy of accounts, systems, procedures, projects etc. Many auditors, as part of their duties, uncover fraud and become involved in the initial and sometimes complete investigation of it. Some auditors become quite specialised in this, and one of them, Peter Tickner, has coined the term 'frauditor' in his book.[3] Another common occupation which becomes involved in investigating frauds is security managers. They usually have a much wider remit than fraud, but it is often one of the criminal risks they become responsible for. Some organisations, because of the volume of frauds they deal with, employ a specialist resource. These are most frequently known as investigators, counter-fraud specialists and fraud examiners.

It is counter-fraud specialists and fraud examiners that the authors believe are the most effective resource an organisation can hire. This is because for this type of personnel, their remit extends beyond investigation to cover prevention, anti-fraud culture work, the pursuit of sanctions etc. In the UK, the qualification and designation that distinguishes this type of fraud professional is the Accredited Counter Fraud Specialist (ACFS). Around 13,000 have received this accreditation in the UK.[4] In America, and increasingly globally, the designation is Certified Fraud Examiner (CFE), which is secured via training with ACFE. They have

50,000 members worldwide, although not all of these will have achieved CFE.[5] The main elements of the exam include:

- Fraud Prevention and Deterrence
- Financial Transactions
- Fraud Investigation
- Legal Elements of Fraud.

This shows how fraud prevention is given significant prominence in the skill set. Many organisations do not have the luxury of being able to afford the full-time capacity of a fraud professional. There are compromises, however. Staff such as auditors can be given specialist fraud training. Organisations can share fraud professionals, or buy in the services of one for a defined number of days per year. In many cases, nevertheless, it will be necessary for an organisation to turn to external expertise to undertake fraud investigations. Two main sources exist: audit/advisory firms such as BDO, KPMG, PKF, PwC etc., and private investigation firms such as Kroll, Carratu, Control Risks, etc. In most countries there are hundreds of firms providing these services, which vary from the large, such as those just mentioned, to some 'one man and his dog operations'. Choosing the best firm for your needs is a significant decision, which requires careful consideration. Some of the issues you need to consider are:

- *Past experience:* Has the organisation got past experience of the type of fraud you have experienced and how successful were they?
- *Reputation:* Have they got a good reputation in appropriate professional circles for conducting this type of work?
- *Capacity, size:* Have they got the depth of staff to conduct the investigation you need? Can they start immediately if that is required?
- *Capacity, functions:* If specialist resources are needed, such as surveillance, computer forensics, forensic accounting, legal sanctions, etc., have they got the capacity to use that type of resource?
- *Capacity, contacts:* If the investigation requires contacts with the police, other law enforcement, regulators, overseas bodies, etc., have they got the capacity and experience for that?
- *Membership of professional bodies:* Are their staff members of appropriate professional bodies such as ACFE, CFPAB, ICFS, accountancy bodies etc.? Are they properly licensed if that is a requirement? Is the firm a member of professional associations?

- *Costs:* Are their costs in the region you can afford?
- *References:* Can they supply details of other organisations that are prepared to testify about their performance?

These are some of the key questions that need to be considered when turning to external help to conduct a fraud investigation. Frequently, help is needed very quickly, and an organisation might rush the decision, which has consequences for the success and costs of the investigation. It is therefore good practice to develop links with a range of bodies that meet your requirements, so that when it is needed, much of the groundwork on the most appropriate body has already been done.

7.4 PROACTIVE INVESTIGATIONS

Returning to Chapter 2 and Figure 2.1, we demonstrated the fraud pyramid with the small number of detected frauds at the top and the larger number of undetected frauds beneath. Many of those types of frauds go undetected or take a long time to be discovered. One means of addressing this is to conduct proactive investigations, to actually go out and search for cases to investigate. This – as has already been mentioned – has a very important preventative role. Maximising detection sends out a clear message to potential fraudsters that if they perpetrate fraud, there is a high chance they will get caught. Some organisations also pursue some of the techniques below in a reactive way, once a suspicion has been aroused. There are a wide variety of tools which can be used to do this.

7.4.1 Data-Matching

Many organisations collect information which is stored in databases and files. Frequently information is collected in these databases which, if matched against other databases, throws up possibilities for further investigation. Data-matching is therefore:

> . . . computerised scanning of data held in different data files either within the same organisation or in different organisations. It can be used by management for a range of purposes including detecting potential fraud.[6]

As an example, within an organisation there is likely to be a dataset of bank account numbers which employees' salaries are paid to. There is also likely to be a dataset of bank account numbers which invoices have been paid to. If you compared those two databases and found several bank account numbers in both datasets, this might be an indication of potential fraud, which requires further investigation. It might be a legitimate case where an employee has an approved external employment/interest which has submitted a legitimate claim to the organisation. It could also be an undeclared interest breaching codes of conduct, or a fraudulent invoice for a front company that a corrupt employee has set up. The data-matching provides a very useful way to compare data to throw up matches for further investigation. Another simple example is comparing whether the same invoice has been paid twice, something which happens quite often in large organisations.

Even more fruitful can be data-matching using data from different organisations. This presents more legal challenges in some countries due to data-protection laws, but it is possible to overcome these. The Audit Commission in the UK has had great success with the National Fraud Initiative. This enables local government bodies to submit various datasets to identify potential areas of fraud. These include checks on entitlement to benefits, tax discounts and sub-letting of council property. In the 2008–9 initiative over £215 million in fraud, overpayments and errors was discovered.[7] A typical example of many of the searches is comparing the number of people registered at a property on the electoral register against properties claiming council tax discount for one person living there.

There are challenges to data-matching, although the power of software is increasingly able to meet some of these. For example, comparing names can pose challenges because of different usages. A David might be listed as Dave on some datasets, or with the middle name as well on others. If exact matches are sought, this might mean that this entry slips through the net. Software can attempt to deal with this, but might then throw up too many false positives. If there are too many of these this can swamp investigators, reducing the potential benefits of the tool.

In the insurance sector in the UK there have been a number of initiatives to enhance the prevention and detection of fraud. The Claims and Underwriting Exchange has details of all claims made in the last five years, enabling multiple claims to be identified. The *Motor Insurance Anti-Fraud and Theft Register* contains details of all vehicles stolen or written off after an accident. The Motor Insurance Database holds data on all insured drivers (including named drivers) enabling checks to be made on who holds motor insurance.[8]

There are a number of companies that specialise in these methods offering a variety of services to organisations to enable data-matching (and mining) to take place. Experian provides a range of services to help prevent and detect fraud. One of the most famous products is Hunter, which is aimed at any fraud involving claims or applications. It works by comparing applications against past applications by that person and/or any past fraudulent applications. It then identifies anomalies for further investigation. Experian provide a case study of the British bank Cheltenham and Gloucester which used Hunter to prevent and detect mortgage fraud. They claim, as a result of using it, some of the following successes:

- Fraud detected increased by 100 per cent;
- More effective detection of fraud with higher density of fraud referrals;
- Savings of £2.4 million of fraud in first week alone; and
- An increase of 36 per cent in the detection of fraud, with reduction in false positive rates.[9]

Another example of a company providing data-matching services is 192business.com (this company has recently been taken over by Experian). One example of a service they provide is identity verification. They provide an example of how the service works for an online retailer: the prospective customer would provide various personal details, which 192business.com would then compare against the electoral roll and other databases. This enables them to produce a report, which the retailer can then act on.[10]

7.4.2 Data-Mining

Alongside data-matching another strategy which can be pursued is data-mining, which can be defined as:

> ... the process of selecting, exploring and modelling large amounts of data to reveal previously unknown patterns, behaviours, trends or relationships which may help to identify cases of fraud. Because of the large amount of data that need to be analysed, specialist computer software is used which usually contain a range of data mining tools.[11]

The principles of this process are to look at data, identify common patterns and then look in more depth at those things which do not fit them. For example, in America, a doctor might make a claim to an insurance provider for fees for treatments to x patients for a certain type of condition. Profiling data across a sector, it will be possible to determine the average number, y, of patients for such a condition treated by a doctor. If x is substantially more than y, this warrants further investigation. It may well be they are more efficient, but it could also be because they are making fraudulent claims. So one of the key approaches of data-mining is profiling data and then finding anomalies. Central to this are statistical tests and distributions. If the size of transactions can be plotted in a normal bell-shaped curve, this enables outliers to be identified and scrutinised. The principles of statistics mean that 68 per cent of values will be within one standard deviation on the curve, 90 per cent of values will be within two standard deviations and 99.7 per cent within three standard deviations. Therefore, if a counter-fraud specialist were to assess a group of transactions, such as overtime payments, once the mean and standard deviation were identified and if the distribution was identified as normal (bell-shaped curve), the specialist could focus upon the outliers beyond two or three standard deviations. There may be a perfectly legitimate reason for some overtime claims between two or three standard deviations more than the mean, but there also might not be![12]

Another common application is Benford's Law. It is worth explaining this in a bit more depth. Probability would lead one to expect that, within a collection of statistics, the chances of picking a number beginning with any given digit would be evenly distributed, i.e. a 1 in 9 or 11.1 per cent chance. However, in reality, with large populations of data this is not the case. Invoices, for example – because of common costs – may congregate around common numbers. Benford's law shows that the chance varies as follows:[13]

Table 7.1 Benford's Law

Digit	Likelihood %
1	30.1
2	17.6
3	12.5
4	9.7
5	7.9
6	6.7
7	5.8
8	5.1
9	4.6

This law is important for data-mining. If an investigation of the payments of invoices was undertaken it should, if profiled, produce a profile not too dissimilar to the above. A fraudster, unless aware of this law, is likely to submit invoices with a different profile. Data-mining can spot profiles of expenditure that don't fit with normal profiles and then the reasons can be investigated further.

There are a variety of more sophisticated data-mining strategies available, some of which will be briefly outlined (for a very comprehensive overview of all the latest data-mining techniques see Mena's book, *Investigative Data Mining for Security and Criminal Detection*, published by Butterworth-Heinemann). Behavioural profiling is based upon the principle that the way a person behaves in a range of areas often provides a unique picture, which can be as useful as DNA. Therefore, once such 'normal' patterns of behaviour can be matched, they can then be used to draw attention to anomalies.[14] Many people will use regular cash machines, purchase within a particular financial range on the credit card, and use the card in particular countries. Differences from the norm can be used to alert staff to conduct further investigations. There may, of course, be a perfectly legitimate reason. Such is the effectiveness of some data-mining techniques, that analysis of credit card transactions can be used to predict to 98 per cent accuracy if a person is going to get divorced.[15]

Text-mining identifies key words and terms associated with a particular area which has been identified at risk, and then searches for these in documents, application forms, claim forms, e-mails etc. So, for instance, if a group of fraudsters applied for credit cards using stolen identities, they might reuse the same language/data on an application form. This, once identified, can then be used to search for others or alert staff.

Another common form of data-mining is link analysis. Once some aspects of a fraud have been identified, investigators can begin to examine the links. This can involve 'people, places, organisations, vehicles, bank accounts, telephone numbers, e-mail addresses ...' to name the most common.[16] These can then be analysed in depth to determine links. Such analysis is often presented in complex diagrams showing lines and linking some of the above. As a simple example, if an insurance company identified a fabricated insurance claim, that fraudster may have made previous claims and used the same address, phone number, bank account, etc. Searches for these details may throw up other claims which can be linked.

7.4.3 Data-sharing and Networking

The sharing of information between fraud professionals has gone on for as long as they have been around. Most commonly this has occurred through informal and formal networks. Some fraud investigators lunch together, or go to the bar and discuss trends, latest scams and fraudsters, amongst many other issues. In more formal settings and professional associations such networking and information sharing also goes on. However, what have emerged over the last 10 years are IT-based tools, which enable much more sophisticated sharing of information. In many countries fraud professionals have developed such tools.

In the UK, the Insurance Fraud Investigators Group (IFIG) is one of the best examples. It provides a range of functions to members, but most importantly it provides a forum to share intelligence amongst members according to the British National Intelligence Model (which will be discussed shortly).[17] So, for instance, if a person makes a fraudulent insurance application, the investigator will log details of this on their database. Other investigators conducting their work might then type in the applicant's name and come up with the prior 'form' of that person logged by other investigators. In America there is a less sophisticated website with similar aims – which has public and member access – called www.insurancefraud.org/index.lasso. On the site, information can be found on those arrested for fraud and convicted for fraud, amongst many other sources.

7.4.4 Intelligence

Intelligence is also important in preventing, detecting and investigating fraud. It is particularly important in organisations which face large numbers of frauds from a diversity of sources, above all, external. It is distinct from information in that it has been analysed for some purpose in an investigation. The Association of Chief Police Officers in England and Wales[18] has defined criminal intelligence as:

> ... the end product of a process, sometimes physical, always intellectual, derived from information which has been collated, analysed and evaluated in order to prevent crime or secure the apprehension of offenders.

In the UK, in the statutory sector, most investigatory bodies work to the National Intelligence Model (or 5x 5x 5x). It has also been used in the private sector to much success, for example by IFIG, as described above. This allows for assessments to be made on the priority of investigations

Table 7.2 The National Intelligence Model

Source Evaluation	
A	Always Reliable
B	Mostly Reliable
C	Sometimes Reliable
D	Unreliable
E	Untested
Intelligence Evaluation	
1	Known to be true without reservation
2	Information known personally to the source but not to the reporting officer
3	Information is not known personally to the source but there is corroboration by information already recorded
4	Information that is not known to the source and cannot be corroborated
5	Information that is suspected to be false
Handling Code	
Code 1	Permits dissemination to other law enforcement and prosecuting agencies including agencies within the European Union where there are sufficient safeguards to protect the rights of individuals
Code 2	Permits dissemination to non-prosecuting agencies (such as credit card companies)
Code 3	Permits dissemination to foreign agencies outside the European Union where no, or inadequate, legal safeguards to protect the rights of individuals exist, however this is only on the grounds of substantial public interest
Code 4	Permits dissemination only within originating agency/force with internal recipients
Code 5	Permits dissemination to other agencies but only in accord with specified conditions such as 'no further dissemination' or 'to be discussed with originator and documented below'

based upon the quality of the information. The model is set out above in Table 7.2.[19] Intelligence received by bodies working to this model is assessed according to the quality of the source (A, B, C, D, E), the quality of the intelligence (1, 2, 3, 4, 5) and is also given a code as to who it can be distributed to.

7.5 REACTIVE INVESTIGATIONS

The detection of fraud in most organisations is still largely the result of reactive measures. ACFE[20] provides very useful data upon where the initial detection of frauds occurred. By far the most important source is tips to counter-fraud professionals, but management reviews and internal audit are also important. The following list illustrates where the initial detection of the fraud occurred by percentage:

- Tip 40.2 per cent
- Management review 15.4 per cent
- Internal audit 13.9 per cent
- Accident 8.3 per cent
- Account reconciliation 6.1 per cent
- Document examination 5.2 per cent
- External audit 4.6 per cent
- Surveillance/Monitoring 2.6 per cent
- Notified by Police 1.8 per cent
- Confession 1 per cent
- IT controls 0.8 per cent

In terms of where the source of the tip originated, employees were by far the most important. Customers, anonymous sources and vendors were also important. The list below illustrates the sources:

- Employees 49.2 per cent
- Customers 17.8 per cent
- Anonymous 13.4 per cent
- Vendor 12.1 per cent
- Stakeholder/Owner 3.7 per cent
- Competitor 2.5 per cent
- Perpetrator's acquaintance 1.8 per cent

The above highlights what was described in Chapter 6 in preventing fraud and creating an anti-fraud culture: the need for well-publicised hotlines and encouraging staff to report suspected fraud. These alone account for a half of all cases reported. The ability to report anonymously is also important given that 13.4 per cent choose to do it in this way.

Once a suspected case arrives on the desk of a fraud professional, they need to plan the way forward. A key decision will be what the potential outcome of the investigation might be. Some organisations which have volume frauds may have clear policies on what the outcome will be. Others who rarely detect fraud may have to convene early meetings with key staff to decide. This decision is very important, since it will influence what the investigators can do, because of the legal regulation of the gathering of evidence for the potential outcomes. The most common outcomes are:

- Criminal prosecution
- Civil suit
- Regulatory sanctions
- Termination of employment
- Finding out what happened.

In most jurisdictions, pursuing a criminal prosecution will involve the most controls on how an investigation can proceed. Civil and employment-aimed investigations will also have controls, but they are generally fewer. Simply finding out what happened, so it can be prevented from happening again, obviously has the fewest. Some organisations will start with the aim of a criminal prosecution orientated investigation, even though this might not be likely, so they at least have the option of doing so.

7.6 CONDUCTING FRAUD INVESTIGATIONS

Once a case has been identified for investigation either by proactive or reactive means, there are a number of strategies the investigator may pursue to secure the necessary evidence to conclude the case. By their very nature most fraud cases will have a 'paper' or 'electronic' trail. That is, the fraudster will have manipulated legitimate documentation (on paper or electronically) to secure an advantage or produced false documentation. Take the classic fraud of an employee setting up a false invoice for non-existent services to be paid by the organisation he/she works for. There will be an invoice, there will be a bank account it is paid to and there will be an authorisation process amongst much more information. Each of these will provide evidence for the investigator once it has been determined it is a false invoice. Compare this to a burglary where, other than forensic evidence, there is unlikely to be much information at the scene identifying who the suspect is. Frauds are different, therefore, from most other volume crimes, in that in many cases once the fraud has occurred and has been confirmed, it is usually relatively easy to determine who did it. Nevertheless, evidence still needs to be secured to achieve the outcome that is the aim of the investigation. Thus a 'desk-based' investigation will provide the spine of the investigation in many cases of checking paperwork, documents and cross-checking with other information sources.[21] The other main investigative techniques will now be explored.

7.6.1 Interviews

In most generic criminal investigations the interview is the most important tool of the investigator. It is used with witnesses to secure information on events they have seen, and to confront suspects to secure their views on what may or may not have happened and particularly to test the validity of what they are saying. With fraud investigations there is often a greater reliance on paper/electronic-based evidence, rather than securing accounts of a particular event. However, interviewing suspects and witnesses is still likely to be necessary. In most jurisdictions interviews of suspects and witnesses for the purpose of a criminal prosecution are heavily regulated. As we have already established, many fraud investigations do not have this purpose, as a civil – or lesser – outcome is the aim. So fraud investigators, in some cases, may be less constrained than those investigators who are only focused upon a criminal outcome. Nevertheless, many start with the aim of keeping all sanctions on the table, which means having to comply with regulations. Compliance also means that the evidence gained is likely to be stronger than if it was gained through other means, even if the outcome sought is not criminal. Therefore there are advantages to complying with the higher standards of interviews set for criminal investigations.

There is also much guidance on good practice in interviewing. Before some of this is briefly explored, some of the problems that have been exposed in interviewing more generally will be identified. For example, interruption of interviewees when they give their first account of an event is generally viewed as bad practice. The first account is likely to be the best and interruption often leads the interviewee to reduce the time of their answer, as they expect to be interrupted. Some research has found interviewees being interrupted on average 7.5 seconds into an interview.[22] Some assessments of interviews have also found lots of short, rapid, unstructured questions, when open-ended questions are seen as best practice. In a study of 600 police interviews, Baldwin[23] found 36 per cent to be of an unacceptable standard with:

- General ineptitude: interviewers nervous and lacking confidence;
- Assumption of guilt: investigators assuming the suspect to be guilty and as a consequence missing some evidence;

- Poor interviewing: lots of interruptions and a failure to grasp key points which needed to be proved;
- Unprofessional: offering inducements and harrying and aggressive in approach.

In the public sector in England and Wales, in response to inadequate interviewing, there has been a huge amount of research and, as a consequence of this, much guidance on good practice in interviewing. For example, the PEACE model of investigative interviewing is advocated in the UK. The key aspects are listed below and further detail can be found in the National Police Improvement Agency's *National Investigative Interviewing Strategy*:[24]

Planning and Preparation

This speaks for itself: to plan and prepare for an interview and not just rush in.

Engage and Explain

Best practice in getting the interview started and establishing the ground rules to be observed.

Account, Clarification and Challenge

Securing the interviewee's account of a particular event, clarifying it and then seeking to challenge it to ascertain the validity of it.

Closure

What needs to be considered before the interview is closed.

Evaluation

This is evaluating the interview in the context of the broader investigation as well as individually in the context of the interviewer's own professional development.

Pursuing the PEACE model is not the only aspect to effective interviewing. Some of the central skills required include good communication skills. The ability to establish rapport with an interviewee is also very important and central to this is empathy. The skill to develop and ask the most appropriate questions, particularly open-ended questions. Understanding non-verbal behaviour is also very important, particularly some of the cues which indicate deception (which will shortly be explored).

All of the above has assumed that the suspect/witness is willing to be interviewed. Most fraud investigators do not possess special powers which can compel a person to be interviewed. However, many CFS have good working relationships with the police, which enable them, once enough evidence has been secured for the police to arrest the person, to conduct the interview.[25] Of course many suspects and interviewees when asked to be interviewed will simply comply. Finally, in certain contexts where there is some form of contractual relationship, there is an expectation to comply with a reasonable request; failure to do so may result in the termination of that contract. This is much more common vis-à-vis search, which will be explored shortly.

7.6.2 Surveillance

Surveillance is a very common tool used in investigations by the police and many other public sector bodies. In the private sector it is also used, but for many there is often a reluctance to do so for fear of the legal implications. In the UK there are three types of surveillance legally defined:

Intrusive: covert surveillance generally undertaken in a residential property or vehicle. Mainly undertaken by the police and other public bodies and requires special approval.

Directed: covert but not intrusive and used to secure private information on a person. Undertaken by police, public and private sectors and approval required depends upon the body and the circumstances.

Covert human intelligence sources: the use of a person covertly to develop relationships to secure information. Undertaken by public and private sectors and any approval required depends upon the body and the circumstances.[26]

For fraud investigators in many investigations there are clear benefits to using surveillance. For example if an insurance firm receives a claim from a person relating to a back injury, but there is doubt, surveillance can confirm or deny this. Thus if a person is followed and they play tennis or go to the gym and footage of this is recorded, this can be useful in repudiating a claim. Similarly, if a company suspects that an employee who is off sick is actually working for another firm, surveillance may secure evidence of them working for another organisation. This type of surveillance is directed and is generally carried out by teams of skilled staff carrying small or hidden cameras, sometimes from specialist vehicles.

Some organisations also resort to using undercover investigators or covert human intelligence sources. If a company suspects there is a section or team who are corrupt and engaged in fraudulent practices, it might be difficult to secure evidence. So to address this, an undercover investigator is sent to infiltrate the group and secure evidence and intelligence.

Undertaking surveillance and using covert sources are very challenging tools for any organisation to use. There are a variety of legal risks; it must be ensured that any activities pursued are lawful. There is also the risk of the tools being discovered and consequent damage to relations, as well as potential legal consequences (if not done properly). There is also a personal risk to those conducting surveillance if discovered. In addition, it may require specialist and expensive equipment. For all these reasons when conducting surveillance it is best to use staff who are highly trained and experienced in surveillance and, if the organisation does not warrant the employment of dedicated staff, it is best to turn to one of the many specialist companies which offer such services.

7.6.3 Searches

Searches are also an important part of investigations and they can cover the physical property of a person, as well as searches of some of the many databases which exist.

(a) Physical

In England and Wales the vast majority of CFS, even where some do have special powers, do not have powers of search. In most cases where a search is required, the CFS will work with the police to provide evidence to support the police in applying for a warrant for a search to take place, which they will pursue in partnership with them. However, there are other routes to conduct searches to enable a CFS to secure evidence.

Many organisations insert clauses in the employment contracts of their employees to enable them to conduct searches. These cannot be forced, but non-compliance with a request could result in disciplinary action, culminating in termination of employment. For many employees who wish to keep their jobs, it is difficult to refuse a search. For employers to insist on a search policy, they need to adopt the express right to do so and link this to clear procedures, which are followed.[27] The most important requirement is for an express clause in an employee's contract of employment, or link to a code of practice, setting out the employer's right to undertake searches and the consequences of refusal. The following extract from a major UK supermarket chain is typical of many.

> 3.14 Searches
>
> The Company undertakes searches as a security measure, both to guard against potential danger and to ensure that unauthorised goods are not removed from the premises.
>
> It is a condition of your employment that you agree to be searched at any time whilst you are on company premises. The search may include your person, anything you are carrying, your desk, your locker, and any vehicle in your charge. You may be stopped outside the boundary of the Company premises and may be invited to return to the building for the purposes of a search. Searches may be carried out by a member of the security staff or a member of the management. Whenever necessary, more thorough personal searches will be conducted in private by a member of your own sex in the presence of another security officer or a member of management.
>
> If it is found that you refused to submit to a search, disciplinary action, which could lead to summary dismissal, will be taken.[28]

There is much advice for organisations to ensure their searches are lawful. The policy on searches should make clear in what circumstances a search may take place, what might be searched, who may undertake the search and the conditions of the search. In terms of the latter, general guidance to employers suggests securing the express consent from an employee such as through the signature to a search authorisation form.[29] To further strengthen the employer's position security staff (or other designated staff) should be properly trained and searches should be restricted (with consent) to the employee's bag, vehicle, pockets and outer clothing. Even with consent it is doubtful if any search which was more intimate would be lawful. To ensure that policies are followed and that there are no allegations of misconduct there should also be a witness to the search.[30] Thus where a CFS is investigating an employee and such a clause exists, a search is a possibility, even off the employer's property.

(b) Information

There is a huge amount of information available publicly either free or for a fee which an investigator can use to secure information. Thus once a suspect has been identified various searches using online databases can quickly be undertaken. In many fraud cases it is important to gain a picture of person's financial position. In most countries it is possible to secure a credit score from a credit reference agency, to search for bad debts, to find out if a person is a director of a company and what property a person owns. There are also databases of all news reports which can be used to search for a person's name. There are companies which specialise in this type of information gathering, but there are many skills an investigator can learn to conduct these types of investigations. Some of the best sources are listed in the box below.

Useful selected tools for securing information on persons/ organisations[31]

Companies and directors

www.companieshouse.gov.uk – basic company information; directors; directors' information; and disqualified directors
www.sec.gov – database of companies registered in the US
www.icpcredit.com – international credit status reports on registered companies.
www.creditcheck.uk.com – a useful database of county court judgements issued against companies.

Courts and legal information

www.courtnewsuk.co.uk – access a vast database comprehensive court and tribunal diary available
www.hmcourts-service.gov.uk – this site lists all the vexatious litigants and the date the order was made
www.casetrack.com – access to a vast database of court and tribunal judgements
www.courtserve.net – daily court lists available
www.trustonline.org.uk – a database containing details of High Court judgements, magistrates' court fines defaults and tribunal awards.

Credit reference

www.uk.equifax.com – UK commercial & consumer credit data

www.uk.experian.com – UK commercial & consumer credit data
www.dbai.dnb.com – UK commercial & consumer credit data
www.trustonline.org.uk – a database containing details of CCJs, Administration Orders and CSA Liability Orders
www.checkmyarea.com – to search any postcode to see geodemographic data
www.insolvency.gov.uk – searchable register of current bankruptcies and Individual Voluntary Arrangements held by The Insolvency Service for England & Wales.

Electoral roll

www.192.com – name and address databases
www.eroll.co.uk – name and address databases
www.tracesmart.co.uk – name and address databases, with a few extra services
www.theukelectoralroll.co.uk – name and address databases, with a few extra services.

Newspaper databases

www.factiva.com – newspaper database
www.highbeam.com – newspaper database
www.lexisnexis.com – newspaper database
www.allyoucanread.com – links to newspapers around the world
www.newseum.org – newspapers from cities from around the world.

People search

www.yasni.co.uk – people search site, very UK focused
www.pipl.com – a comprehensive people search engine
www.wink.com – a search engine for individuals by name, location and interests
www.yoname.com – check an individual against a number of the most popular social networking sites
www.searchirc.com – check a name or nickname against a number of chat rooms and other sites
www.123people.com – 123people is a search engine that searches just for people, checking documents, social networking groups and directories
www.peekyou.com – PeekYou searches for people on various social networking sites, groups and directories
www.spokeo.com – Spokeo searches for people on various social networking sites, groups and directories

www.namechk.com – check to see if a username is used at dozens of popular social networking and social bookmarking websites.

Image search

www.tineye.com – a reverse image search engine, useful for linking images on social networking sites.

Property

www.voa.gov.uk – searchable database of the Valuation Office, listing all residential & business properties in England & Wales. There is also a list of certain residential rental properties

www.landregisteronline.gov.uk – ownership database for properties in England & Wales.

Telephone

www.infobel.com – worldwide telephone directories

www.phonebooks.com – worldwide telephone directories

www.btexchanges.com – BT directory enquiries in the UK

www.ukphonebook.com – UK directory enquiries and other UK databases

www.phonepayplus.org.uk – the premium rate services regulator, with a database for checking premium rate numbers

www.whocallsme.com – if you received a strange call, most likely you are not the only one. Search for this phone number to see the reports of others

www.saynoto0870.com – non-geographical alternative telephone numbers for companies

www.numberingplans.com – some useful online tools linked to mobile phones

www.gsmarena.com – mobile terms glossary & links to phone manufacturers, where each phone's capabilities are listed.

Vehicle

www.webuyanycar.com – if you enter a registration number it will give details of vehicle make, colour, engine size, date of first registration etc and also a photograph of the model

www.national.co.uk – National Tyres offer a service called 'Find My Tyres' – if you enter a registration number it will give details of vehicle make, colour, engine size etc

www.hpicheck.com – vehicle checking service

www.mycarcheck.com – vehicle checking service, covering stolen and write-off reports which are charged for, but basic make and model details from the registration number are free
www.rac.co.uk – basic vehicle checking service
www.taxdisc.direct.gov.uk – click on Vehicle Enquiry and if you have the registration number and make, you can do a vehicle check and get a lot of the information from the log book apart from the keeper details
www.ukcampsite.co.uk – stolen caravan & motorhome database
www.registerstolenplant.co.uk – stolen plant and equipment register
www.numberplates.com – data base of how different countries vehicle registration plates are formatted
www.frixo.com – free live road traffic reports.

General source of useful sites and databases

http://www.uk-osint.net/favorites.html

Thus, it is possible to secure a huge amount of information on a person or company from these types of sites. There is also of course the growing resource of social networking sites. These can provide useful information about a person's career, education, etc., as well as their lifestyle.

7.6.4 Forensics

Television programmes such as CSI have highlighted the huge potential of different forensic techniques for the police, largely in murder investigations. Forensics also has its use in fraud investigations and is used by both public and private bodies. Indeed most of these techniques are available on the open market, provided by a variety of companies which specialise in these tools for a price. Document analysis, fingerprints, substance analysis, DNA services can all be purchased by organisations. IT forensics can also be utilised so that data can be retrieved from computers, laptops, mobile phones, etc. Even equipment which has been damaged and/or data which have been deleted can be retrieved by some experts. For most organisations the employment of a CSI department is too expensive. Thus, for most organisations access to these services is sought on a case-by-case basis, weighing up the economics of the case.

It is therefore very important to select companies with proven expertise, success and appropriate accreditations to conduct this type of work.

7.7 PSYCHOLOGY AND INVESTIGATION

There is a growing body of literature from the discipline of psychology, which can greatly aid the investigator. The most significant is the literature on detecting deception or the telling of lies. When an investigator interviews a suspect or a witness, the ability to identify whether they are telling the truth is a very important skill. Unfortunately there is much research to suggest that investigators (largely police officers) are generally not very good at identifying liars.[32] The ability to undertake this task is not helped further by lots of manuals which identify a range of cues which may indicate a person is lying, but as Vrij argues:

> . . . there is no cue a lie detector can ever rely upon. This does not mean that cues to deception never occur. They do occur, but different people may display different cues to deceit, and the same person may display different cues in different situations.[33]

To use the analogy of Pinocchio, there is no cue equivalent to his expanding nose. However, this is not to dismiss psychology as offering any help to the investigator, because there is much that can be learnt from the literature, which when applied gives the investigator a greater chance than the lay person in detecting lies. Lying is generally more cognitively demanding than telling the truth. The following illustrates why:[34]

- Creating the lie may involve cognitive demands, such as fabricating the details to make the lie convincing.
- Someone telling the truth is unlikely to be worried about their credibility, whereas a liar will be.
- The concern with credibility is likely to mean the liar will monitor the interviewer more carefully, to see if they are getting away with it.
- Liars may be more concerned over their acting and role-play.
- Liars need to hide the truth.
- Activating a lie requires more effort than telling the truth.

One can see that lying is therefore more cognitively demanding than telling the truth. There are a variety of cues which indicate cognitive load, and which can be used to help determine if a person is more likely to be telling the truth. Some of the most prominent identified by Vrij et al.[35] are listed below.

7.7.1 Verbal Cues

When someone has to describe an event in detail this is often very demanding for a liar, as they often lack the ability to fabricate the finer details. There are tools such as Criteria-Based Content Analysis and Reality Monitoring, which assess the number of details made in a statement, such as visual (what was seen), audio (what was heard), contextual (details of location) etc.[36]

7.7.2 Vocal Cues

There are numerous vocal cues associated with higher cognitive load. These include increased latency (time lapse between question and answer), a larger number of pauses between words and sentences, greater hesitation ('um', 'uh' etc.), a larger number of speech errors (grammatical, false starts, etc.), and a slower speech rate.

7.7.3 Visual Cues

Increased cognitive load is also associated with a decrease in certain types of movements and neglect of body language. Researchers have suggested increased load will lead to fewer 'illustrators' such as hand/finger movements, eye blinks, leg/foot movements and chair swivels.[37]

There are a wide variety of other cues which may be associated with increased cognitive load and lying. For a consideration of these it is worth reading Vrij's book, *Detecting Lies and Deceit*.

7.7.4 Experiments Increasing Cognitive Load

If lying is associated with increased cognitive load, then measures to further increase that load may exaggerate the load and therefore expose more cues to make detecting liars easier. There have been a number of experiments to prove this. In one experiment where truth-tellers and liars were asked to recall events in reverse order, it was found that liars exhibited more examples of cognitive load. Police officers were able to detect more liars using this technique, with a 60 per cent accuracy rate compared to 42 per cent when told in the normal order.[38]

In another experiment with pairs of liars, they were presented with unanticipated questions, such as spatial (where in relation to the front door did you sit) and temporal (in which order did you discuss the topics mentioned earlier). When pairs plan lies, there are only a limited number of scenarios they can rehearse. So posing something they are unlikely to have considered is likely to expose inconsistency. Thus, they may not have considered where they actually sat in a restaurant, and both will have to guess, increasing the chances of exposing inconsistency. An experiment examining this found that liars gave more inconsistent answers to unanticipated questions.[39]

The above two experiments represent only a fraction of the research available, which can be used to help expose liars in a wide range of contexts. Vrij identifies 17 techniques to improve the chances of catching a liar:[40]

1. Use flexible decision rules: don't assume one cue indicates lying – use the broader base of knowledge to apply to the particular case.
2. Bear in mind that cues for deceit are most likely to emerge when a person experiences cognitive load, emotions or attempts to control themselves.
3. Consider alternative explanations when interpreting cues: remember a person may be nervous or there may be other explanations for the cues exhibited.
4. Be suspicious but do not show suspicion: showing suspicion may make truth-tellers uncomfortable, leading them to exhibit cues.
5. Do not make up your mind too quickly on whether a person is lying.
6. Pay attention to the more diagnostic verbal and non-verbal cues.
7. Pay attention to verbal and non-verbal cues simultaneously.
8. Pay attention to the deviations from a person's honest reactions in similar situations: the comparable truth.
9. Employ indirect lie detection techniques: for example ask a person if the suspect is thinking hard rather than whether they are lying.
10. Use an information gathering interview style.
11. Detecting deception may be easier in the first interview.
12. Be informed about the factual evidence.
13. Let the person repeat themselves.
14. Let interviewees elaborate.

15. Ask temporal questions when a scripted answer is suspected.
16. Make interviews more cognitively demanding.
17. If evidence is available use it strategically.

The above is a short précis of what can be gleaned from Vrij et al.'s work on detecting deception. Ultimately it is a difficult skill to learn and there is much research which needs to be digested. Nevertheless, although it will never be possible to develop approaches which have 100 per cent or near detection rates, it is possible to substantially shift the odds in favour of the person seeking to detect deception.

7.8 CONCLUSION

This chapter has considered the detection and investigation of fraud. It began by illustrating the expense of investigating fraud and why it is better to try and prevent it in the first place. It then moved on to examine the issues that need to be considered when selecting an external firm to conduct an investigation. Proactive measures to investigate and detect fraud were then examined, including: data-matching, data-mining, data-sharing and intelligence. The chapter then moved on to consider reactive investigations, exploring the evidence of where many of them originate. The strategies to investigate were then outlined, including desk-based strategies, interviews, surveillance, physical searches, information searches and forensics. Finally, the chapter considered what psychology research has to offer in helping the fraud investigator detect deception.

Model Detection and Investigation Strategy

Data-matching
Data-mining
Data-sharing and networking
Intelligence
Interviewing using PEACE
Using surveillance when necessary
Utilising legal tools to search
Maximising the potential for online search
Utilising psychological research to enhance the detection of deception

FURTHER READING

Mena, J. (2003) *Investigative Data Mining for Security and Criminal Detection*. London: Butterworth-Heinemann.

Milne, B. and Bull, R. (1999) *Investigative Interviewing: Psychology and Practice*. Chichester: John Wiley & Sons.

Tickner, P. (2010) *How to be a Successful Frauditor*. Chichester: John Wiley & Sons.

Vrij, A. (2008) *Detecting Lies and Deceit*. Chichester: John Wiley & Sons.

For sources on online information sources which may aid investigations go to http://www.uk-osint.net/favorites.html.

END NOTES

1. The Guardian (2010) *MP's Expense Abuse Investigation Tops £500,000*. Retrieved 18 August 2011 from http://www.guardian.co.uk/politics/2010/mar/30/mps-expenses-abuse-inquiry-500000.
2. Holtfreter, K., Van Slyke, S., Bratton, J. and Gertz, M. (2008) Public Perceptions of White Collar Crime and Punishment. *Journal of Criminal Justice*, 36: 50–60; Calavita, K., Pontell, H. and Tillman, R. (1997) *Big Money Crime: Fraud and Politics in the S and L Crisis*. Irvine: University of California Press.
3. Tickner, P. (2010) *How to be a Successful Frauditor*. Chichester: John Wiley & Sons.
4. Button, M., Johnston, L., Frimpong, K. and Smith, G. (2007) New Directions in Policing Fraud: the Emergence of the Counter Fraud Specialist in the United Kingdom. *International Journal of the Sociology of the Law*, 35: 192–208.
5. ACFE (n.d.) *Welcome to the World's Leading Anti-Fraud Organisation*. Retrieved 18 August 2011 from http://www.acfe.com/.
6. NAO (n.d.) *Good Practice Guide. Tackling External Fraud*. London: NAO, p. 10.
7. Audit Commission (n.d). *National Fraud Initiative Reports 2008–9*. Retrieved 18 August 2011 from http://www.audit-commission.gov.uk/nfi/news/Pages/nationalfraudinitiativereports200809.aspx.
8. ABI (n.d.). *Tackling Fraud*. Retrieved 27 November 2007, from http://www.abi.org.uk/Display/default.asp?Menu_ID=1140andMenu_All=1,946,1140and Child_ID=458.
9. Experian (n.d.) *Case Study: Cheltenham and Gloucester*. Retrieved 18 August 2011 from http://www.experian.co.uk/assets/consumer-information/brochures/C&G_CS_v1.pdf.
10. 192 Business (n.d.) *Identity Verification*. Retrieved 18 August 2011 from http://www.192business.com/our-solutions/verification/identity.
11. NAO, op. cit., p. 33.
12. Tickner, op. cit.
13. Tickner, pp. 27–28.
14. Mena, J. (2003) *Investigative Data Mining for Security and Criminal Detection*. London: Butterworth-Heinemann.

15. Armstrong, S. (2011) Will You Get Divorced? Your Credit Card Knows. *Sunday Times*, 27 March, 2011, p. 7.
16. Mena, op. cit., p. 75.
17. IFIG (n.d.) *Closing in on the Cheats*. Retrieved 18 August 2011 from http://www.ifig.org/.
18. Association of Chief Police Officers (ACPO) (1975). *Report of the Subcommittee on Criminal Intelligence* (The Baumber Report). London: Association of Chief Police Officers, para. 32.
19. Adapted from Sheptycki, J.W.E. (2004). *Review of the influence of strategic intelligence on organised crime policy and practice (Special Interest Paper 14)*. London: Home Office.
20. ACFE (2010) *Report to the Nation on Occupational Fraud and Abuse*. Austin: ACFE.
21. Smith, G., Button, M., Johnston, L. and Frimpong, K. (2010) *Studying Fraud as White Collar Crime*. Basingstoke: Palgrave.
22. Milne, B. and Bull, R. (1999) *Investigative Interviewing: Psychology and Practice*. Chichester: John Wiley & Sons.
23. Baldwin, J. (1992) *Video-taping Police Interviews with Suspects: An Evaluation*. London: Home Office.
24. National Police Improvement Agency (2009) *National Investigative Interviewing Strategy*. Retrieved 7 February 2011 from http://www.npia.police.uk/.../National_Investigative_Interviewing_Strategy_09.pdf.
25. See Button, M. (2011) Fraud Investigation and the 'Flawed Architecture' of Counter Fraud Entities in the United Kingdom. *International Journal of Law Crime and Justice*. 39: 249–265.
26. See http://surveillancecommissioners.independent.gov.uk/advice_definition.html.
27. Baker, N. (1999) Searching Employees. *Croner Employment Digest* 487: 4–6.
28. Search and Seizure Files Institute of Personnel and Development Library.
29. Croner Employment Digest (1992) May I Look in Your Bag? *Croner Employment Digest* 355: 1–3.
30. Ibid.
31. These are drawn from http://www.uk-osint.net/favorites.html which has the most comprehensive list of tools.
32. Vrigh, A. (2008) *Detecting Lies and Deceit*. Chichester: John Wiley & Sons.
33. Ibid, p, 374.
34. Vrigh, A., Mann, S.A., Fisher, R.P., Leal, S., Milne, R. and Bull, R. (2008) Increasing Cognitive Load to Facilitate Lie Detection: The Benefit of Recalling an Event in Reverse Order. *Law and Human Behaviour*, 32: 253–265.
35. Ibid.
36. Ibid.
37. Ibid.
38. Ibid.
39. Vrij, A., Leal, S., Granhag, P.A., Mann, S., Fisher, R.P., Hillman, J. and Sperry, K. (2009) Outsmarting the Liars: The Benefit of Asking Unanticipated Questions. *Law and Human Behaviour*, 33: 159–166.
40. Vrigh, op. cit., chapter 15, pp. 396–417.

8

Sanctioning Fraudsters and Pursuing Redress

8.1 INTRODUCTION

In many ways, when the stage of sanctions and redress has been reached, it is an illustration of failure, because clearly the best situation is to have prevented the fraud in the first place. However, as this book has shown, there is much fraud which does occur and when it does, it's important to get all or as much as possible of the money back, as well as to punish that fraudster. The latter is not just important from a moral perspective but also for the purposes of individual and general deterrence. For many lay observers, sanctions centre around the criminal justice system. However, this masks the fact that fraud can also be a civil tort. As will be shown in this chapter, the criminal approach is one of many other types of sanctions which can be used against fraudsters. These centre around disciplinary (where they are an employee), civil and regulatory sanctions too. Most importantly these can also be pursued in parallel. Ultimately, the victim has a choice to pursue a number of options, of which criminal sanctions are only one. This chapter will begin by examining the importance of deterrence, before moving on to examine the sanctions toolbox in more depth and the benefits and disadvantages of different approaches. Before this is considered, however, it is important to note that in criminological literature the most important factor in influencing criminals' decision-making is their likelihood of getting caught.[1] Therefore, the strategies outlined in Chapter 7 on detection and investigation are just as important as any sanctions applied in securing deterrence.

8.2 UNDERSTANDING FRAUDSTERS AND THE PLACE OF DETERRENCE

In most organisations there will be frauds discovered and then investigated, which culminate in the need for a decision on what to do with the fraudster. The sanctions which can be applied could vary from nothing to a combination of criminal, civil, regulatory and disciplinary sanctions. What organisations do varies considerably, often for very similar frauds.[2] It is important to understand the motivation of some fraudsters and the significance of both deterrence to them from engaging in further fraud and general deterrence to a wider group of sanctioning that particular fraudster, as well as the desire to recoup some or all of the losses from the fraud.

Underpinning many of the arguments in this chapter is the work of Braithwaite and his regulatory pyramid, where action to secure compliance starts with persuasion and then gradually escalates up the pyramid to more punitive sanctions such as a warning, civil sanction and criminal prosecution.[3] Where those persuasive strategies have failed, sanctions become appropriate. It is also important to note the importance of sanctions in deterrence. This can be divided between individual deterrence and general deterrence. In the former, sanctions are applied with the aim of deterring that individual from engaging in the sanctioned form of behaviour again. In general deterrence, the aim is to publicise the sanctions applied to the individual, with the aim of deterring anyone in that organisation, region or society from thinking of or engaging in that type of behaviour, or from pursuing such behaviour if they are already engaged in it. There is much debate and research on how effective sanctions are for different types of behaviour in securing deterrence. McGuire[4] has noted the following key observations, that for deterrence to work, the sanctions must be:

- Inevitable and unavoidable
- Administered immediately or speedily
- Of high to maximum severity.

Potential offenders must consider that the sanctions will be more or less inevitable and unavoidable if they engage in certain behaviour. Thus, for a fraudster to take note, they must think that there is a very good chance they will get caught and that sanctions will be very likely. Second, there must be a perception that if caught, the sanctions will be applied relatively speedily. Third, that the sanctions applied will be of a level that is severe. Unfortunately in many jurisdictions one cannot state that sanctions fit the above three criteria for fraudsters.

Many fraudsters are not caught, or take a long time to get caught. Indeed, in some countries there is police disinterest or lack of resources for the detection of fraudsters. This is mirrored in many organisations where inadequate resources are available for the detection of fraudsters.

Second, when frauds are dealt with by the criminal justice system there is often a long time lag before the case is held. For some complex frauds the preparation for trial and the trial itself take a very long time. Finally, the penalties imposed on fraudsters are often not very severe, particularly when compared to 'comparable crimes' as was illustrated in Chapter 4.

Sanctions have a very important place in a counter-fraud strategy for the following reasons:

- to provide the top of the regulatory pyramid;
- to provide individual and general deterrence;
- to provide a means for the victim to get all or some of their money back;
- to maintain public confidence in the organisation concerned.

8.3 THE SANCTIONS TOOL BOX

There are different types of sanctions which can be pursued against a fraudster, some by decision of the relevant court or tribunal, others by an organisation. The most common are listed below:

- sanctions involving the application of the criminal law;
- sanctions involving the application of the civil law;
- regulatory sanctions to prevent an organisation or an individual (often a member of a 'profession') undertaking work similar to that undertaken while the fraud took place; and
- disciplinary sanctions to remove a fraudster from the context of their fraud, so that they cannot repeat what they have done.

The important issue to note is that the criminal law is not the only route to sanctions. There are many others. The full list of sanctions available in England and Wales are listed in the two boxes below.

Non-Criminal Sanctions

Staff disciplinary: staff could be suspended, demoted or sacked.

Withdrawal of services: if the fraudster is receiving services such as insurance cover and the fraud involves the insurer these services could be withdrawn.

Informal warnings: low level frauds could result in an informal warning with a statement that if repeated more serious sanctions could be applied.

Name on fraudsters' database: there are a number of databases operated, such as the CIFAS databases, and confirmed fraud could result in placement upon them. This has implications for employment and access to certain services.

Administrative penalties: in some sectors because of special legislation it is possible to apply administrative penalties for low level frauds.

Civil penalties: amongst retailers it is common for fraudsters and other low level criminals to be issued with civil penalties, which are letters demanding payment for losses, costs of investigation, etc.

Freezing orders: if civil litigation is pursued it is common to secure a freezing order so that the fraudster cannot spend or hide their assets. Although not a form of punishment, the restrictions these place on an individual could be seen as a sanction.

Civil suit: the fraudster can be sued in the civil courts to recover losses and costs.

Contempt of court: if the fraudster ignores or breaches the requirements in a civil case they could be pursued for contempt of court, which carries possible fines and lengthy jail sentences.

Regulatory sanctions: if the fraudster holds a licence or other instrument to conduct their work engaging in fraud often puts that at risk. The fraudster could therefore be targeted for sanctions through a regulatory body.

Anti-Social Behaviour Orders (ASBO): these are civil orders which prescribe a certain type of behaviour, breach of which is a criminal offence. Certain types of repetitive fraudulent behaviour could be targeted with one of these.

Serious Crime Prevention Orders (SCPO): these are similar to ASBOs but for more serious crimes, including fraud.

Criminal Sanctions

Formal caution: a formal caution from the state.

Restraint order: similar to freezing order above but for criminal cases.

Upon conviction:

- *ASBO* (can be applied post-conviction too)
- *SCPO* (can be applied post-conviction too)
- *Compensation order* (order to pay compensation to victim)
- *Restitution order* (order to return property to victim)
- *Deprivation order* (order to take away artefacts which could be used for further crimes)
- *Confiscation order* (confiscation of property secured through criminal gains)
- *Financial reporting order* (order to supply financial information)
- *Disqualification from acting as a Company Director*
- *Disqualification from driving*
- *Community order, curfew order* and *imprisonment*

The criminal process in nearly all cases requires the support of the state to investigate (or at least validate the investigation which has been undertaken) and to initiate prosecution. Unfortunately this is not always available. The best way to secure police interest in many cases is to produce a file of evidence according to their requirements. At one extreme this could be a complete package which can be handed over to the police for validation and passage to the prosecutors. It could also be a package to stimulate police interest to become more actively involved, or to secure their interest to conduct searches, which usually require their support. Some organisations also put on the table the willingness to pursue a private prosecution. Then the police are often more interested because if the CPS say no, they know there will be a fall-back position which means their time has not been wasted. The pursuit of a private prosecution can also be used to trigger CPS interest in taking over the case, which is possible in England and Wales (although they can also take over to discontinue).

The decision over which route or routes to take also has implications for evidence gathering, with many more controls on this in the criminal process. Ultimately the choice of sanctions to pursue will depend upon the circumstances of the victim and the nature of the fraud. Further consideration of this will be undertaken shortly.

8.3.1 Quasi-Sanctions

Other 'quasi-sanctions' can also have a significant effect on the fraudster, but are 'applied' more informally. For example for many white collar criminals, which includes many fraudsters, research has shown shame is a very important factor. Merely knowing that others know one has been engaged in criminal activity is seen as more devastating than any criminal justice punishment. For example in one study, which looked at petty theft, drink driving and tax evasion, for the latter the threat of shame of family, friends, colleagues, etc. knowing was the most important threat.[5]

Such informal penalties can be created by promoting selected cases which have been proven through the media. Fraudsters and potential fraudsters will see the impact of such publicity on the attitudes of the community in which they live. They will also see the ongoing reduced chances of prosperous employment and its impact on the quality of life of the fraudster and those close to him or her. The fear of such informal sanctions as a deterrent should not be under-estimated.

The extent to which such sanctions are applied effectively is key in deterring the repeat of similar behaviour, not just by the specific fraudster on whom the sanctions are applied, but by others who may contemplate fraud.

A prevalent view of fraud is that society divides into three main groups in its attitude to fraud: those who are irredeemably honest, those who are irredeemably dishonest, and those who are opportunists. The estimated size of these three groups varies, but it is usually agreed that the 'opportunist' group is the largest. That being the case, it is important that they are deterred by their perceptions of the risks involved in undertaking fraud.

The risks concerned do not solely concern sanctions. For example, if there is no fear of detection, there will be no fear of a sanction being applied. Other factors which can help to create a strong deterrent effect include:

- the extent to which there is peer group pressure indicating that fraud is socially unacceptable;
- the extent to which there is a perception that there are strong systems in place to prevent fraud if it is attempted;
- the extent to which there is a perception that, if fraud is attempted, it is likely that it will be detected; and
- the extent to which it is believed that a suspicion of fraud will result in a professional, thorough investigation which will uncover evidence of what has happened.

It is sometimes assumed that it is the severity of the sanction which is most important in its deterrent effect, but this is only one element of what is important. The experience of the UK NHS Counter Fraud Service between 1998 and 2006 was that it was the proportionality and certainty of the sanctions that had the greatest impact.

If a sanction is not likely to be applied then the perceived risk will be low. If the severity of the sanctions in place is such that they are only seen to be proportionate in serious cases, then they will not deter lower value fraud. The most effective solution is a range of flexible sanctions which are seen to have a high chance of being applied across the full range of potential fraud.

8.3.2 The Main Formal Sanctions

Let us return to the main sanctions which can be applied:

- criminal sanctions;
- civil legal sanctions;
- disciplinary sanctions; and
- regulatory sanctions.

These vary in detail across different jurisdictions. To consider the detail of particular statutes or provisions in individual countries would inhibit the general approach of this book, which is to highlight generic ways in which the financial cost of fraud can be reduced across the world. It is also the case that the different categories of sanctions operate in a remarkably similar fashion. What is important is to consider the different sanctions and the part that they can each play in countering fraud.

Criminal sanctions exist primarily to punish the individual, with sentences including imprisonment and fines. Compensation can also be sought upon conviction. The threat of criminal prosecution can also be very useful in getting fraudsters to hand over assets. The civil law is used to trace and freeze assets and to recover losses. The reality of most civil cases is that they are settled before the court case. For instance Mr X has defrauded £30k from his employer and is detected. Before confronting him, the company freezes his assets and then negotiates with Mr X. Often, a deal is done where Mr X reimburses the company before the case actually comes to the civil courts. Of course in some cases it doesn't. It is also worth noting some of the very useful tools available through this route which can be used.

Useful Civil Orders/Tools[6]

The High Court can issue injunctive relief for those seeking to preserve the assets of those they are seeking a claim against. It is also important to note that these can be secured out of working hours from a judge. Some of these are listed below.

Freezing orders

This is an interim order, which prevents the removal of assets from a jurisdiction and/or the dealing with assets. This is usually limited to assets matching the value of the claim.

Asset disclosure

Part of the freezing order can include a requirement for the defendant to disclose all their assets.

Travel restrictions/Passport order

Orders can be made restricting travel and compelling the defendant to give up passports and travel documents until they have complied with asset/tracing information.

Gagging orders

These prevent the defendant disclosing to third parties the details of freezing orders.

Search orders

Search orders can be made which permit the claimant's agents to enter the defendant's office(s), home(s) and car(s) to search for and seize documents or property.

Disobeying the order amounts to contempt of court and can result in imprisonment for the defendant.

Disciplinary sanctions, which are probably the most common, include dismissal, or a lesser sanction such as demotion, suspension, etc. Regulatory sanctions are applied to prevent an organisation or individual continuing to operate, especially where an individual has breached the technical or ethical standards of their profession.

Traditionally, there has often been a 'silo' approach to the application of sanctions, with no apparent attempt being made to combine them. Even the traditional language of fraud has not helped. By describing fraud as a 'crime' we appear to state that it is nothing more than that, whereas it may also be the subject of civil legal proceedings, and disciplinary or regulatory action.

Again, traditionally, the criminal law has had precedence, despite criminal prosecutions having the toughest standards of proof ('beyond reasonable doubt') and the most complex evidential and procedural requirements. Many cases of fraud fail to be successfully prosecuted because of such difficulties, where they might well have been successfully taken forward in the civil courts.

The historical precedence of criminal law has also delayed the pursuit of other types of sanctions in some cases – with losses not recovered pending the outcome of a long criminal investigation and professional and employment status not being addressed promptly, despite the strength of the case.

Over the past decade or so this has started to change. In particular, the development of a legally obligatory 'parallel sanctions' policy in the UK National Health Service,[7] and its being supported by the UK Attorney-General in a subsequent large scale case (Operation Holbein against pharmaceutical companies), helped to change the position and to open a new debate. 'Parallel sanctions', that is, a requirement to consider undertaking criminal, civil, disciplinary and regulatory sanctions at the same time rather than sequentially, is still a legally binding Government requirement in the English NHS. Some of the parallel sanctions will now be explored in the English context – but it is highly likely that such combinations are also available in many other jurisdictions, particularly those based upon the common law. Clearly, however, as with any legal issue, those in other countries should consult lawyers upon their options relating to parallel sanctions.

8.3.3 Possible Parallel Sanctions

The following briefly examines some of the dilemmas relating to parallel sanctions and what is possible. For more detailed explanations of the justification for these statements readers are referred to the publicly available NHS Counter Fraud Service Guidance *Applying Appropriate Sanctions Consistently.*[8]

(i) Dismissal before outcome of criminal or civil case

The most common dilemma for many organisations where an employee is found to have committed fraud is whether that person can be disciplined and/or sacked before the outcome of the trial. Clearly, if they are suspended and the case lasts a long time, this could be a substantial additional burden upon the organisation, on top of the fraud losses already incurred. The key issue is for the employer to follow the usual disciplinary procedures, which should comply with appropriate regulations and legislation. As the NHS guidance notes:

> There is nothing to prevent an employer conducting a disciplinary enquiry if criminal charges are being considered or a criminal investigation is in progress, as long as the process is conducted fairly and in accordance with the employer's disciplinary procedures.[9]

There may even be some cases, where the employee is caught 'red handed' and confesses, where a detailed investigation into the case is not even required. This would still mean, however, that the disciplinary/dismissal procedures would need to be followed.

(ii) Civil before criminal?

Another dilemma for many organisations is if they want to pursue a fraudster criminally: do they have to put off any civil claims until this is complete? The NHS guidance drawing upon extensive case law is also very clear upon this issue:

> The general approach of the courts since the late 1970s has been *not* to give automatic precedence to the criminal proceedings but, on the contrary, to postpone other forms of proceedings *only* if there is evidence of a real danger of prejudice to the interests of the individual in running their criminal defence.[10]

Based upon past experience of court cases for most frauds, it is possible for the victim to pursue redress through the civil courts before the criminal case.

(iii) Admissibility of evidence

Parallel cases become very complicated when considering the admissibility of different forms of evidence for different cases. For example, in some civil cases there is a requirement for a defendant to answer questions. There is no such compulsion in a criminal case. Such evidence gained under the civil process cannot be used in a criminal case. For interviews in criminal cases there are extensive rules concerning how they should be conducted under the Police and Criminal Evidence Act 1984.

Many disciplinary and civil cases involve interviews not conducted under such regulations. This affects the admissibility of such evidence for criminal cases.

The important issue to grasp is that this is a complex area which requires expertise. Those pursuing parallel investigations need to utilise people with appropriate expertise from a very early stage and communicate with one another. A good starting point for a consideration of such issues is the NHS guidance.[11]

Considering the above, let's now imagine an accountant who has defrauded his company of £100,000. Let's also imagine that they have lied about their past, and have been dismissed from a previous company for fraud. If the organisation wanted to inflict the maximum punishment on this person what could they do?

- Terminate their employment
- Freeze their assets
- Pursue a civil claim for losses and the costs of the case
- Enter their name on a fraudsters' database such as the CIFAS database
- Pursue a criminal prosecution which may result in imprisonment or other penalties
- Seek an ASBO or SCPO preventing them from holding out to be an accountant
- Pursue disciplinary action via the regulatory body for accountants, with the aim of having them struck off
- Publicise the case in the media.

This is a very wide range of sanctions and could not be considered light. The publicising of this in the media could also have a substantial deterrent effect upon others, which is what we turn to now.

8.4 PUBLICISING SANCTIONS

Earlier, the informal sanction of shame was raised. Central to raising that as a sanction is the publicising of cases. In most cases it is also important to publicise the sanctions which have been applied to fraudsters. In some cases there might be agreements for no publicity, or there may be reputational issues which mean it is unwise to publicise. The importance of publicity is to foster the anti-fraud culture by demonstrating that people do get caught, and that what happens to them as a consequence is not nice. Publicity to achieve this can be pursued at a number of levels:

- Highlighting of cases in fraud awareness training
- Publication of cases in newsletters
- Release of information to the media to encourage coverage.

A good example of this approach is the Hampshire and Isle of Wight monthly *Fraud Matters* newsletter. This provides a range of information relating to fraud, but most significantly it contains a regular collection of NHS staff who have been involved in fraud and the consequences of their action. The box below contains an extract from one such case publicised in the newsletter.

Practice manager jailed for stealing £267k from GPs[12]

A former practice manager has been sentenced to three years' imprisonment after defrauding her employers of £267k, following an investigation by NHS Protect.

Ms X managed a medical centre for 10 years. Between April 2007 and November 2009 she paid herself an extra £108,615.17 in salary plus £159,244.40 in overtime that she was not entitled to . . .

From when she started at the surgery in 1999, one of her duties was to oversee its payroll, which on her recommendation was outsourced in 2005. Ms X ensured she was the sole point of contact, so the payroll provider would deal only with her. As profits fell and the practice struggled to pay its tax bill, the partners repeatedly asked Ms X for financial data, which she claimed was not available.

When they insisted on seeing salary spreadsheets, she created false ones. The partners had to take out loans and mortgages to keep the practice afloat, and could not afford to replace staff. Ms X resigned and left the practice in November 2009, after being challenged about poor timekeeping and her sickness absence record. In her final month, she tried to cover her tracks by paying herself the appropriate salary in line with Agenda for Change pay scales.

The extent of her fraud was identified in February 2010 by two doctors at the practice. She handed herself in to the police and was arrested. The Metropolitan Police and NHS Protect collaborated on the investigation.

8.5 CONCLUSION

The pursuit of sanctions is an important part of the overall counter-fraud strategy. They are important in underpinning some of the other strategies as well as in securing deterrence and in recovering losses. Ideally, an organisation should hold a 'full toolbox' and be prepared to use all of those tools – depending upon the circumstances. Organisations should also not shy away from pursuing parallel sanctions where they want to give a clear message that fraud will not be tolerated and that consequences will be very severe. The chapter provides an 'agenda for change' to make the application of sanctions easier, more effective and more impactful on the fraudster. This is one important factor in deterring fraud, changing human behaviour and reducing the cost of fraud.

Model Sanctions Strategy

Detect and investigate as many cases as possible
Keep open as many sanctions as possible: criminal, civil, regulatory and disciplinary
Keep open the possibility of parallel sanctions
Use informal sanctions
Publicise cases

FURTHER READING

Button, M., Lewis, C., Shepherd, D., Brooks, G. and Wakefield, A. (2012) *Fraud and Punishment: Enhancing Deterrence through More Effective Sanctions*. Portsmouth: Centre for Counter Fraud Studies.

NHS Counter Fraud Service (2007) *Applying Appropriate Sanctions Consistently*. London: NHS Counter Fraud Service.

END NOTES

1. Farrington, D.P., Ohlin, L.E. and Wilson, J.Q. (1986) *Understanding and Controlling Crime*. New York: Springer Verlag.
2. NHS Counter Fraud Service (2007) *Applying Appropriate Sanctions Consistently*. London: NHS Counter Fraud Service.
3. Ayers, I. and Braithwaite, J. (1995) *Responsive Regulation*. Oxford: Oxford University Press.

4. McGuire, J. (2002) Criminal Sanctions versus Psychologically-based Interventions with Offenders: A Comparative Empirical Analysis. *Psychology, Crime and Law*, 8: 183–208.
5. Grasmick, H. and Bursik, R. (1990) Conscience, Significant Others, and Rational Choice. *Law and Society Review*, 24.
6. NHS Counter Fraud Service (2007) op. cit.
7. Ibid.
8. Ibid.
9. Ibid, p. 8.
10. Ibid, p. 6.
11. Ibid.
12. Hampshire and Isle of Wight Counter Fraud Service (2012) *Fraud Matters*. Issue 31, March 2012. p. 4.

9

Enhancing Performance through Counter-Fraud Metrics

9.1 INTRODUCTION

This book has set out many strategies to enhance the fight against fraud. However, it is not enough to just have a counter-fraud strategy and to be doing the 'right' thing. What is also required is a minimum standard of performance and targets to increase that performance over time. Key Performance Indicators (KPIs) have become common in some parts of the public sector in the UK and beyond. However, KPIs represent only a partial contribution towards creating competitive advantage. KPIs that focus significantly upon costs, or metrics, as they are more commonly known, are also needed. In this chapter we outline how a programme of metrics can be applied to countering fraud, how to set up a programme as well as some of the potential limitations one has to be careful about when creating such a system. Before we embark upon this, however, we explore the context to them and what metrics are.

9.2 NEW WAYS OF THINKING ABOUT SECURITY AND FRAUD

There have been growing debates in security management and, to a lesser extent, counter-fraud during the noughties, concerning models of delivering security and counter-fraud services.[1] The traditionalist paradigm of delivery in security and counter-fraud is a reactive model dealing with detected problems. Structures to deliver these services are considered as a necessary cost on the business, and as offering little in contributing to the overall aims of the organisation. In short, they are a necessary service for which a minimal level of cost has to be set aside. In security and counter-fraud these approaches are often associated with former police, service personnel and other service functions which have to host them, such as facilities, audit, finance, etc. In the traditional paradigm there are often no metrics or performance indicators at all. Rather, the department is given a general remit and it is up to the discretion of the management and staff how it fulfils this role. The further down the hierarchy one goes leaving managers and counter-fraud specialists to determine where they think they should concentrate their time and resources, the more likely it is that there will be increasing differences from what those at the top actually expect them to do.[2]

Without clear measures of performance, however, it is difficult for such entities to demonstrate their contribution to an organisation and to see how well they are doing. For many counter-fraud entities without a clear set of metrics, it leads to challenges when increasingly financially focused organisations in both the private and public sectors begin to ask some of the following questions:

- What is the counter-fraud department/section costing me?
- What do I get for my money?
- Does it work?
- How do you know it is working?
- Can it be done at lower cost?
- If something went wrong, why did it go wrong and what wasn't working?

Without some form of programme of KPIs or metrics this is hard to address. In response to this, as well as other agendas, in many areas of the public sector in the UK (and parts of the private sector) KPIs have become very common. These measure various areas of performance. A very traditional set of KPIs for a fraud entity in the public sector are the KPIs for the Royal Borough of Windsor and Maidenhead set out in Table 9.1 below.

Another example is from Croydon where the performance is actually set against the target. Table 9.2 shows that, in terms of the YTD, the performance is two below the target on sanctions and some £50,000 below on identified overpayments and savings.

The above are sound basic indicators of performance, but they tell us little about what the overall counter-fraud department of these boroughs is contributing towards the bottom line, other than the value of the detected fraud/overpayments. As we have discussed extensively in this book, this provides only part of the picture. Some organisations have embraced the term 'metric', but not necessarily the 'modern metrics'

Table 9.1 KPIs for Royal Borough of Windsor and Maidenhead for Benefit Fraud[3]

Description	2006/07	2007/08	2008/09	2009/10
Number of benefit fraud referrals	491	474	397	239
Number of cases investigated and closed	304	399	230	86
Number of cautions	7	10	2	3
Number of administrative penalties	23	33	26	14
Number of prosecutions	7	18	24	7 (9 pending)
Value of fraud overpayments identified (LA) / £	460,000	557,000	349,638	175,050
Value of fraud overpayments identified (DWP) / £	0	0	158,684	21,604
Value of administration penalties / £	23,000	21,000	12,443	6,474

approach. For example, the UK Identity and Passport Service has a series of 'performance metrics'. One of the headline metrics is:

> To reduce our level of undetected application fraud to below 0.08% of passport applications.[4]

This is reported on a monthly and yearly basis. In reality this is more a KPI rebadged as a metric. There is therefore room for the reform of KPIs to provide a more value orientated measure (this is not to say that this is an issue which should not be subject to a metric/KPI). This is where metrics have developed. Before we examine metrics it would be useful to put this third type of approach in broader context of how some writers have been thinking about security and counter-fraud.

Table 9.2 Selected KPIs from Croydon Council[5]

	Target		Performance
	YTD	Annual	YTD
Sanctions	30	120	28
Identified overpayments and savings	£300,000	£1,200,000	£250,289

In the late 90s and early 00s, some writers and practitioners have begun to challenge traditional models of delivery of counter-fraud and security. Some reformers have argued for more business-like approaches, where there is much more focus on what security and counter-fraud can do to the bottom line. Briggs and Edwards[6] have argued that business orientated models of security could actually reap a 'new competitive advantage'. Gill et al.[7] have identified the advantages and attractions of so called 'new entrepreneurs' in delivering security, rather than 'traditionalists'. One of the authors has developed these arguments further, calling for Security Risk Management.[8] In the NHS, the Counter Fraud Service pioneered a model of delivering counter-fraud that focused upon the return on investment in investing in countering fraud. Underpinning all of these reformist agendas is an approach that seeks to more accurately measure the impact, performance and costs of security and counter-fraud. Central to this are metrics.

Metrics and security metrics have become more common in the business world, insurance industry and computer security.[9] In recent years there has been growing interest in physical security management and, to a lesser extent, counter-fraud. These and other factors have encouraged some to argue for greater use of security metrics in the more general security management field (physical, human, financial security systems, etc.) Most think of metrics as some form of measure. This is correct, but metrics are more than simple measures. Swanson[10] defines metrics as:

> ... tools designed to facilitate decision making and improve performance and accountability through collection, analysis, and reporting of relevant performance-related data. The purpose of measuring performance is to monitor the status of measured activities and facilitate improvement in those activities by applying corrective actions, based on observed measurements.

It is the periodic assessment of the same metrics over time which distinguishes them from measures. Another important aspect of them is that they are used to inform organisational decision-making. Their other defining characteristic is the focus upon value and costs. Metrics are very common in modern business organisations, and the few listed below give a flavour of the types of metrics used:

- Freight cost per mile (total expenditure on freight divided by mileage)
- Cost per square foot (total warehouse operating costs divided by size)

- Website conversion rate (percentage of unique visitors to website who buy something)
- Average revenue per user (ARPU).

In the broader security world there has been growing interest in applying metrics to security. Given the overlap and parallels between counter-fraud and security, there is much to be learnt from this literature. Kovacich and Halibozek[11] argue that security metrics are:

> The application of quantitative, statistical, and/or mathematical analyses to measuring security functional costs, benefits, successes, failures, trends, and workload – in other words, tracking the status of each security function in those terms.

As mentioned above, some areas of 'generic' corporate security have already gone down the route of pursuing security metrics, such as retail security. However, probably the most significant area where security metrics have emerged is computer security.[12] Interest in and use of metrics in the world of IT has spawned an extensive literature on security metrics, which provides many lessons for counter-fraud metrics.

It is also important to note the influence of performance management more generally, particularly in the public sector.[13] This has spawned a general interest in indicators of performance (and critiques of it). Another important influence is the growing interest in 'convergence'.[14] This is a business model that seeks to merge different loss protection functions such as risk and compliance – and within that computer, physical and people based security, etc. – together. This clearly highlights weaknesses in some traditional models of security when compared with computer security, and debates begin to emerge about how performances in addressing risks are measured. To summarise, approaches to performance in counter-fraud can be distinguished into three broad ideal types:

- *Traditional discretion*: no clear set of regular measures of performance; instead left to discretion of management and staff, who may publicise measures on an ad hoc basis.
- *Traditional KPI*: clear set of performance indicators, but they have little reference to costs and value.
- *Modern metrics*: clear set of metrics linked to costs and value.

9.3 DEVELOPING A COUNTER-FRAUD METRICS PROGRAMME

Now the context of the emergence of metrics has been considered, it would seem appropriate to explore the process of developing a counter-fraud metrics programme. Payne[15] has identified seven steps to developing a metrics programme. They are:

- Define overall objectives/metrics
- Decide metrics that meet those objectives
- Develop strategies for generating metrics
- Establish benchmarks and targets
- Determine how metrics will be reported
- Create action plan
- Establish formal review/refinement cycle.

Payne wrote these with a computer security program in mind. These can be easily adapted to counter fraud. Each of these will now be considered:

9.4 DEFINE OVERALL OBJECTIVES/METRICS

The first stage is to identify the broad objectives of a counter-fraud entity. These are foundations upon which the finer metrics are then constructed which contribute to these broad objectives. A traditional example adapted from a local authority is set out below:

> The primary function of the Benefit Fraud Service is to prevent, detect and investigate potential/suspected fraudulent claims for Housing Benefit and Council Tax Benefit in accordance with the Social Security Administration Act 1992, other legislative requirements and the Council's Anti-Benefit Fraud Strategy and Policy.[16]

A more 'Modern metrics' orientated approach for a company would be as follows:

> The objective of the Counter-Fraud Department is to reduce fraud to an absolute minimum without compromising the core objectives of the company, and to provide a return on investment for the company for the investment in counter-fraud resources within 3 years.

We will explore later the type of metrics which could follow on from such a statement.

9.5 DECIDE METRICS THAT MEET THOSE OBJECTIVES

Once the broad objective has been set, the next challenge is to create a series of metrics that can contribute to meeting that broad objective. There are a number of different types of metrics which could be considered. These are set out in the box below.

Types of metrics

Strategic

The team may wish to establish strategic metrics which enable long-term decisions to be made regarding the allocation of resources, such as comparisons between the costs of fraud losses over time.

Quality assurance

More quality focused metrics may be considered to ensure consistency of service delivery. For example: are appropriate numbers of proprietary checks conducted, are they of suitable quality, or what is the number of staff who have been to fraud awareness training?

Tactical

Metrics focused upon a particular problem to help develop a tactical solution may also be considered. For example, does advertising a fraud hotline lead to an increase in the number of usable tips? This data can then be used to influence tactical decisions on deploying counter-fraud resources.

Qualitative versus quantitative

It would be wrong to assume that the nature of metrics makes qualitative measures unsuitable. Many organisations may wish to focus upon subjective qualitative measures, such as attitudes to fraud and corruption. These can be converted to ordinal numbers which enable metrics to be developed.

Contemporary/lagging

When developing the mix of metrics, it may also be important to examine the needs for the timeliness of metrics, whether to have contemporary or lagging metrics. For example, how many cases of fraud occurred yesterday, rather than in the last quarter?

'Fuzzing' measurement of impact of fault injection into a system

A common practice in computer security is 'fuzzing'.[17] This is the deliberate introduction of faults into the security system to test the consequences for security. For example, what happens when a piece of anti-virus software is disabled? This could also be used in counter-fraud. For example, in the area of expenses fraud a particular control could be removed for a period of time to assess the impact upon levels of fraud.

Risks/strategies

Some metrics may be focused upon the actual risks faced, such as number of frauds, breaches of code of conduct, etc. Others might be focused upon the strategies, such as number of investigations, criminal prosecutions, sanctions applied, redress achieved, etc.

Reported versus surveys

Finally, some metrics may be based upon actual incidents, others upon surveys. For example, as was illustrated earlier in this book, fraud loss measurement exercises are the most effective mechanisms to measure fraud. Surveys which assess a representative sample of transactions and then identify them as fraudulent or not are considered to be much more accurate. Thus, if one was seeking to use a metric to measure fraud in an organisation over time, surveys are the best gauge.

As mentioned earlier, in computer security metrics have become much more dominant in security decision-making. Table 9.3 below demonstrates how an example from computer security could be adapted.

Table 9.3 Learning from Computer Security Metrics

Computer security perimeter defence	Counter-fraud insurance fraud metrics
Number of emails per day	Number of claims per day
Number of spam emails detected (stopped) per day	Number of fraudulent claims detected per day
Number of spam emails not detected per day	Number of fraudulent claims not detected per day (via fraud loss measurement exercise)
Detection failure rate	Detection failure rate

Adapted from Herrmann[18]

A useful strategy from the key performance indicator literature which can be used for counter-fraud metrics is the acronym SMART:

- Specific: the metric should be specific and not too general
- Measurable: it should be possible to measure it
- Attainable: any target related to it must be attainable
- Repeatable: it should be repeated to enable comparison
- Time dependent: it should be linked to a time period.

The 'Modern Metrics' approach requires costs and value to be integrated as well. So $ also needs to be added:

- $ Cost and value: should be integrated where possible.

Therefore it becomes SMART $.

9.5.1 Influences

It is also important to note there will be other significant influences shaping the metrics to be created. Broader organisational/corporate objectives will play a part. Thus, if the organisation has profitability as a high priority, metrics related to the bottom line will be important. Whereas, if justice and minimal fraud are important, costs and impact on revenues will not be as central.[19] In many contexts there will be a tension between cost/profit versus justice/minimum fraud. If the culture is dominated by reduced costs and profit, this may be at the expense of the other. For example, in the field of security, Gill[20] found one retailer replacing the arrest of shoplifters with simply stopping shoplifters and seizing stolen goods as it was a far more cost effective solution for the retailer. In the fraud arena some organisations such as the NHS have pursued civil penalties where the culprit pays a fine for low level frauds, rather than pursuing a criminal prosecution. The broader risk management process will also be important. The nature and shape of risks and what needs to be done about them are clearly going to impact upon what is measured. Finally, in varying contexts the regulatory standards will also influence the metrics. For example, in the financial services sector in most countries there is extensive regulation, which often extends to fraud related issues. Compliance with these could also be set as metrics.

9.5.2 Sample Counter-Fraud Metrics

Set out below are a series of sample counter-fraud metrics, which should provide the skeleton counter-fraud metrics for an entity, and which could be adapted and built upon to create a comprehensive set of metrics for an organisation. Before these are explored, however, it is important to set out a hypothetical general objective of a counter-fraud entity in a commercial, profit seeking organisation. Let us return to the one created above:

> The objective of the Counter-Fraud Department is to reduce fraud to an absolute minimum without compromising the core objectives of the company and to provide a return on investment for the company for the investment in counter-fraud resources within 3 years.

There are a series of metrics which could fit below this. We start with the most important 'fundamental metrics'. To enable many other metrics to be created it is important to know the total expenditure upon counter-fraud resources. In some organisations this might be more difficult to undertake because of staff spending a proportion of their time on counter-fraud duties, and because of the difficulty of disentangling certain expenditures. Nevertheless, it is possible to achieve this. The total losses in $ terms for an organisation do present even greater challenges as Chapters 2 and 5 have already shown. First of all, the detected losses can be added to the total. Then where fraud loss measurement exercises have been conducted for certain types of expenditure these can be added. If there are significant areas of expenditure where no prior fraud loss measurement has been conducted, then, unless an estimate is applied based upon other comparable measurement exercises, this total estimated figure will also represent an underestimate. Once an estimate of total losses has been made, it is then possible to calculate the total return on investment from investment in counter-fraud resources (see Table 9.4).

ROI is commonly used in making decisions on different types of investment in organisations, but rarely used in countering fraud. In its simplest form ROI is:

$$\text{ROI} = \frac{(\text{Gain from Investment} - \text{Cost of Investment})}{\text{Cost of Investment}}$$

Table 9.4 Core Counter-Fraud Metrics

Metrics	Time Period
Expenditure on counter-fraud resources	1 year
Total $ losses from fraud detected and estimated	1,2,3 + year basis
Total return on investment of counter-fraud resources	1,2,3 + year basis

Specifically applied to fraud this would be:

$$\text{ROI} = \frac{(\text{Reduction in Fraud Losses \$} - \text{Expenditure on Counter-Fraud resources})}{\text{Expenditure on Counter-Fraud Resources}}$$

As an example, if a $100 million per year organisation with an above average fraud loss rate of 8 per cent ($8 million per year fraud losses) invested $500,000 in counter-fraud resources over a two year period and the rate had reduced to $6 million by the end of year 1 and $5 million by the end of year 2, the reduction in fraud losses would be $5 million minus the $500,000 invested which would be $4.5 million divided by $500,000 which would equal 9. So the return on investment over a two year period would be 9 (where organisations pursue redress these gains can also be added to the gain from investment).

It must be noted that calculations of ROI are fraught with difficulty in seeking to accurately measure the gain and the costs. For example, the gain may be accounted for by factors other than the actual investment. The complexity of the organisation and the type of investment must therefore be borne in mind when undertaking this approach.

9.5.3 Scale of the Problem Metrics

There are a variety of metrics which are important in gauging the size of the problem. Some of the most common are listed below (see Table 9.5). The FLR and FFR and actual $ equivalents are very important and have been discussed already in Chapters 2 and 5. The numbers of detected frauds is also important as well as usable tips to a hotline.

Table 9.5 Scale of the Problem Metrics

Metrics	Time Period
Fraud Loss Rate – Cost of fraud by type of expenditure as a percentage (by statistical sample from fraud loss measurement exercise)	1,2,3 + year basis
Related to above £value reduction in losses since previous measure.	
Fraud Frequency Rate – Number of fraudulent transactions as a percentage (by statistical sample from fraud loss measurement exercise)	1,2,3 + year basis
Number of detected frauds	Monthly to annual
Number of usable tips to hotline	Monthly to annual

Table 9.6 Quality Metrics

Metrics	Time Period
Number of companies within group scoring 40/50 or more on fraud resilience checks	2 + year basis.
Number of company locations scoring 40/50 or more in fraud resilience checks	2 + year basis.

9.5.4 Quality Metrics

In Chapter 4 the resilience of organisations to fraud was discussed. The authors have developed fraud resilience assessment tools, which produce scores indicating the quality of fraud resilience out of a maximum of 50 points. These measures could be used or adapted to assess different companies, organisations in a group, divisions within a company or even broken down to a departmental level. Two examples are given in Table 9.6, one for a large holding company with lots of sub-companies and the other for a large company/body with multiple large sites employing large numbers of staff spread geographically.

It is possible to create a resilience check and scoring system that is tailored to the organisation's needs. However, having a set of metrics related to this is useful in judging overall quality.

9.5.5 Prevention Metrics

It is important to distinguish between the different aspects of a counter-fraud strategy and apply metrics to these too. The first metrics relate to prevention and anti-fraud culture. Evaluation of systems to prevent fraud is important. The number of staff attending fraud awareness training, the number of such sessions conducted and the number of positive stories in the media are some examples of many more which could be utilised (see Table 9.7).

Metrics could also delve into the strength of the anti-fraud culture amongst staff, particularly their perceptions of the likelihood of getting caught. Some possible metrics which could be developed are listed below (many of these would need to be developed through regular research):

- the strength of peer group pressure indicating that fraud is unacceptable;

Table 9.7 Prevention Metrics

Metrics	Time Period
The number and proportion of process or systems weaknesses where fraud has taken place, which have subsequently been resolved	Annual
The number and proportion of new processes and systems which have been evaluated to identify potential weaknesses	Annual
Number of staff attending fraud awareness training	Monthly to annual
Number of fraud awareness training sessions conducted	Monthly to annual
Total number of positive media stories published relating to counter-fraud	Monthly to annual

- the perceived strength of preventative processes;
- the perceived likelihood of detection;
- the perceived professionalism of those undertaking the investigation and likelihood of evidence being uncovered;
- the extent to which it is felt likely that an effective sanction will be applied; and
- the extent to which potential fraudsters think that any money which they obtain through fraud will be recovered.

Awareness of the risk among potential fraudsters is crucial, and thus publicity is key. Other areas of activity (see below) will provide the 'ammunition' for publicity, but if what is happening is not publicised then potential fraudsters will not be aware of the risks that they face.

Thus, the strength of a deterrent effect is best measured by the number of staff and contractors who will have read communications on this subject. A simple index would involve the number of staff multiplied by the number of communications that they will have read.

9.5.6 Detection and Investigation Metrics

Focusing on the cost of fraud, the key issues in the effectiveness of fraud detection work are how much fraud has been detected and how quickly this has happened after fraud has been initiated. The first issue can be addressed simply by recording the number of cases which have come to light. The second issue can be considered by recording how long a fraud had been taking place before it was detected. This second factor

Table 9.8 Detection and Investigation Metrics

Metrics	Time Period
Number of cases of fraud detected	Quarterly
Where fraud has been found to be present, the average length of time that fraud has continued before detection	Quarterly
Total number of fraud cases investigated	Quarterly
Percentage of detected fraud cases investigated	Quarterly
£value of fraud and unlawful action identified and stopped	Annual
$value of detected fraud cases not investigated	Annual

is very important, obviously, in terms of the extent of the losses which are incurred.

The number, speed and quality of investigations are the most important issues in this area. Measuring the number of investigations which have been commenced and concluded is straightforward, as is reporting on the average duration of those investigations which have been concluded. The third metric has been found to be harder to define satisfactorily. The most commonly accepted metric that has been applied is the proportion of investigations where a conclusion is reached, i.e. where fraud is found either to be present or not present. It is right to comment at this point that metrics in this area generally shed less light than in some other areas of action. Nevertheless, in terms of driving good performance, the authors believe that the right behaviours will be encouraged by the metrics described above.

Some useful metrics to gauge the performance of the investigation team include the number of cases investigated. This could be applied to the number detected, which gives a useful indicator of the percentage of cases that have been investigated. Related to this, it is useful to demonstrate the value of frauds investigated and stopped. Similarly, it is useful to gauge the level of cases which have not been investigated because of resource issues (see Table 9.8).

9.5.7 Sanctions and Redress Metrics

Finally, there are a range of sanctions-related metrics which can be used. The total number of criminal and civil, as well as disciplinary sanctions can be measured. Recoveries of losses in $ can also be recorded (and built into the ROI where appropriate) (see Table 9.9).

Table 9.9 Sanctions and Redress Metrics

Metrics	Time Period
Total number of confirmed cases of fraud where no sanctions have been pursued	Annual
Total number of cases where a criminal prosecution was sought and the proportion which have been successful	Annual
Total number of cases where civil legal action was initiated and the proportion which have been successful	Annual
Total number of cases where disciplinary action was sought and the proportion which have been successful	Annual
Total losses recovered from fraudster	Annual

The above are only showcase metrics and some organisations are likely to build upon these further with many more.

9.6 DEVELOP STRATEGIES FOR GENERATING METRICS

Once the appropriate metrics have been identified the next challenge is to identify strategies to actually generate those metrics. This also poses a series of challenges, not least in accurately collecting and then analysing the data. For example, if one wanted to collect data for a metric on the number of staff who have failed to declare reportable interests, this might pose challenges. First of all, some staff may be deliberately seeking to hide interests and second, some may not realise they need to declare certain interests. One would probably be left with a detected rate, which, as we have discussed already, is likely to represent the tip of the iceberg.

Clearly, modern technological systems can greatly aid the generation of metrics. Retailers with bar coding systems can measure stock losses much more accurately. Tracking systems of goods in transit can also help. With these, the challenge becomes the securing of the investment to gain such a system or influence over one. There are also companies that specialise in developing systems that enable complicated analysis, which is often termed 'analytics'.

For some potential metrics which require special projects to be undertaken, sometimes by independent auditors, such as satisfaction surveys or fraud risk measurement exercises, there is the challenge of not only the cost, but the competency of those who actually do it. For example, for a fraud risk measurement exercise to be taken seriously certain statistical techniques and confidence levels need to be ensured; this requires specialist skills, for which many security departments do not have the capacity in-house.

Another serious question is: how often are the metrics to be generated? Clearly this depends upon the type, but whichever it is, their generation is likely to involve time and resources, and organisations will need to be carefully attuned to the actual need to have the metric versus the implications for resources in generating it.

9.7 ESTABLISH BENCHMARKS AND TARGETS

Metrics alone are of limited use if they are not set against targets and benchmarks to enhance performance. This creates a number of challenges for the decision-maker. Primarily, there is the challenge of not setting the target so high as to skew all measures towards it to meet it at the expense of others, versus setting it so low as to make it meaningless. Some organisations are big enough to benchmark across different departments located in different areas. Some operate in sectors where benchmarking is possible across organisations, particularly in the public sector. However, such is the competition in some areas of the private sector that many would be unwilling to share and compare such data. There are also some sectors where there are actual standards set that need to be adhered to. However, examples of the research from the Centre for Counter Fraud Studies do provide some basis to benchmark some of the 'fundamental metrics'. Organisations can benchmark their FLR against general rates and specific sectors where that analysis has been undertaken, such as healthcare and the public and private sectors.

9.8 DETERMINE HOW METRICS WILL BE REPORTED

Another challenge is actually reporting counter-fraud metrics. The challenge is not just how they are reported, but to whom. If there are many metrics in a department, documents with large numbers of statistics may be a turn-off to many. If the metrics are to be reported beyond the department to the board, this may make accurate interpretation of them difficult. A crucial question will also be how widely all metrics are disseminated, which will depend upon the organisational context. There is much debate in the security metrics literature on the merits of graphs, diagrams, summary sheets and the use of colour. For example, a common approach is to have a summary sheet on one piece of paper with all of the metrics colour-coded: red, amber, green; where red is significantly off target, amber, off target; and green on target. Whichever strategy is used, it is important to report the metrics in a way tailored to the needs of a particular audience.

It is very important, however, to have support at the highest level. Therefore having board consideration of counter-fraud metrics on a regular basis is the best way to ensure that the problem continues to be taken seriously. Providing at least a one-side summary sheet, with some of the skeleton metrics described above set against targets with the traffic light reporting system provides a simple but effective way to monitor performance and ensure board interest.

9.9 CREATE ACTION PLAN

Once the metrics and the targets have been set, the challenge is then to develop an action plan so that they are met. So if, for example, they are reported on a quarterly basis and some metrics are coming up red, the task is then to redeploy resources or change the strategy so that the metric returns to green. This will always sound simpler that it actually is. For example, returning it to green may require additional resources, which the organisation is not prepared to give. It might mean moving resources, which has a detrimental effect elsewhere. Recreating a new strategy might be hard to sell to existing staff, or they might not be capable of moving to it. Nevertheless, it is obviously important to have an action plan to ensure that any reds or ambers return to green.

9.10 REVIEW/REFINE CYCLE

Linked to the above, more radical reviews will need to be undertaken regularly. The process of review may mean that targets which are easily being met need to be upped, or conversely, those which are impossible to meet need to be reduced. The review process may highlight the need for certain targets to be dropped or new ones introduced. This type of review is important to undertake on a periodic basis.

9.11 CHALLENGES AND CRITIQUE OF METRICS

The discussion so far has hinted at a number of challenges in the metrics process. This section will now seek to draw out some of the more general criticisms and challenges of developing a metrics programme.

9.11.1 Distorting Behaviour

One of the most damning criticisms of metrics is that they distort behaviour. Some organisations become so focused upon the metrics that they neglect some of the other things they do which don't have a metric.[21] This is why it is very important to develop an appropriate number of manageable metrics which accurately reflect the objectives of the counter-fraud department. It is therefore important to keep the metrics used under review and to cull and add where appropriate.

9.11.2 'Drowning in Metrics'

Another challenge is that some organisations develop so many metrics that they 'drown in them'. Clearly, there are only a finite number that an organisation can concentrate upon. If too many emerge this may simply lead some organisations to concentrate on some, rather than all, of the metrics. As stated above, it is therefore important to review the metrics regularly, and cull and add where appropriate, to meet the department's and organisation's needs.

9.11.3 Differences in Interpretation Reporting/Recording

Another problem that arises is differences in the interpretation and recording of metrics. For example, there are a number of issues which are subjective in interpretation. For example, in some areas of counter-fraud, staff may be subjected to threats and actual violence by those they are investigating. Verbal abuse, anti-social behaviour and even threats of violence may be interpreted differently by different people. If similar behaviours are interpreted differently, then metrics to measure them will not be based upon the same criteria.

9.11.4 Fiddling

Such is the pressure in some organisations to meet targets it may lead some to engage in fiddling or lesser tactics to meet the metric. Such approaches might include the non-reporting of events, discouragement of reporting by third parties, reassigning incidents, or even completely fabricating data.[22] The integrity of the metrics needs to be beyond doubt and regular audits should be undertaken to ensure the risks of this occurring are minimised.

9.11.5 Costs

For any security metrics programme there will be costs. At the very least it is going to take staff time from performing front-line duties. If investment in technology is also required to implement a programme there could be an additional cost here. So decision-makers will need to do a cost–benefit analysis of whether the implementation of part or all of a security metrics programme is worth it.

9.12 CONCLUSION

This chapter has provided an introduction to the subject of counter-fraud metrics. It has shown how these are central to countering fraud for competitive advantage. The chapter started by linking metrics to new ways of thinking about security and counter-fraud. It illustrated some of the metrics which are currently used by some organisations, before moving on to illustrate how a counter-fraud metrics programme can be developed. Finally the chapter explored some of the problems which can occur with the introduction of metrics or KPI based strategies.

FURTHER READING

Briggs, R. and Edwards, C. (2006) *The Business of Resilience*. London: Demos.
Gill, M. (ed) (2006) *The Handbook of Security*. Basingstoke: Palgrave.
Gill, M., Burns-Howell, T., Keats, G. and Taylor, E. (2007) *Demonstrating the Value of Security*. Leicester: Perpetuity Research.

END NOTES

1. Challinger, D. (2006) Corporate Security: A Cost or Contributor to the Bottom Line. In Gill, M. (ed), *The Handbook of Security*. Basingstoke: Palgrave; Gill, M., Burns-Howell, T., Keats, G. and Taylor, E. (2007) *Demonstrating the Value of Security*. Leicester: Perpetuity Research and Consultancy International; Button, M. (2008) *Doing Security*. Basingstoke: Palgrave.

2. Button, M. (2008) *Doing Security*. Basingstoke: Palgrave; Wagg, C. (2010) *The Campus Sentinels*. BSc Dissertation, University of Portsmouth.
3. The Royal Borough of Windsor and Maidenhead (n.d.) *Key Performance Indicators – Benefit Fraud*. Retrieved 12 April 2012 from http://www.rbwm.gov.uk/web/audit_benfraud_performance_indicators.htm.
4. Identity and Passport Service (n.d.) Untitled. Retrieved 12 April 2012 from http://www.ips.gov.uk/cps/rde/xchg/ips_live/hs.xsl/1021.htm.
5. Croydon Council (2010) *Anti-Fraud Report – April to June 2010*. Retrieved 12 April 2012 from http://www.croydon.gov.uk/contents/documents/meetings/546436/915496/2010-09-07/aa20100907anti-fraud2010.pdf.
6. Briggs, R. and Edwards, C. (2006) *The Business of Resilience*. London: Demos.
7. Gill et al., op. cit.
8. Button, 2008, op. cit.
9. Gill et al., op. cit.; Jaquith, A. (2007) *Security Metrics*. Upper Saddle River (NJ): Pearson Education.
10. Swanson, M., Bartol, N., Sabato, J., Hash, J. and Graffo, L. (2003) *Security Metrics Guide for Information Technology Systems*. Gaithersburg: National Institute of Standards and Technology. Retrieved 12 April 2012 from https://skydrive.live.com/?cid=7086a6423672c497&id=7086A6423672C497!114.
11. Kovacich, G.L. and Halibozek, E.P. (2006) *Security Metrics Management*. Oxford: Butterworth-Heinemann, p. xxvii.
12. See Jaquith op. cit. Herrmann, D. (2007) *Complete Guide to Security and Privacy Metrics*. Boca Raton (FL): Auerbach.
13. Loveday, B. (2006) Policing Performance: The impact of performance targets on police forces in England and Wales. *International Journal of Police Science and Management*, 8: 282–292.
14. KPMG (n.d.) *The Convergence Challenge: Global Survey into the Integration of Governance, Risk and Compliance*. Retrieved 12 April 2012 from http://www.kpmg.com/Global/en/IssuesAndInsights/ArticlesPublications/Pages/The-convergence-challenge-Global-survey.aspx.
15. Payne, S. (2006) *A Guide to Security Metrics*. Retrieved 12 April 2012 from http://www.sans.org/reading_room/whitepapers/auditing/guide-security-metrics_55.
16. The Royal Borough of Windsor and Maidenhead (n.d.) *Benefit Fraud Service*. Retrieved 12 April 2012 from http://www.rbwm.gov.uk/web/audit_benefit_fraud_service.htm.
17. Payne, op. cit.
18. Hermann, op. cit.
19. See Button, op. cit., chapter 6.
20. Gill et al., op. cit.
21. Loveday, op. cit.
22. Ibid.

10
The Counter-Fraud Professional

10.1 INTRODUCTION

This chapter will consider the importance for an organisation – whatever the size – of employing a counter-fraud professional. This may seem like an extravagant expense, but there are a variety of economical models which can be used to achieve this aim. For example, small organisations can contract in the services of a professional for a selected number of days, depending upon their needs, or they can train a member of staff to take on these responsibilities in addition. For medium to larger organisations, the risks of fraud are likely to warrant much more investment in the resource, ultimately culminating in a full-time position or multiple positions. There is no 'one size fits all' and clearly the size, complexity and nature of fraud risks vary significantly between organisations. This chapter will consider what counter-fraud professionals look like and the professional infrastructure, and consider some of the changes required to enhance this. It will also consider what the skill-set of the counter-fraud professional should be.

10.2 COUNTER-FRAUD PROFESSIONAL INFRASTRUCTURE

Throughout this book a wide range of strategies have been advocated to create the best solutions to counter fraud and lead ultimately to competitive advantage for the organisation. Underpinning all of this is having (whether employed directly or via a contract) an appropriate counter-fraud professional (or professionals – depending upon the size of the organisation) to lead the fight against fraud. In most organisations the focus of counter-fraud activity usually centres around reactive investigations and developing controls. These are only part of what is required, as the chapters of this book have shown. Most commonly counter-fraud responsibilities are allocated to one or more of the following, depending upon the size and nature of the organisation: auditors, investigators or security managers. In the more enlightened organisations, these more general staff develop a fraud expertise and secure specialist fraud qualifications. In some organisations, such is the size and/or the fraud risk that they employ specialist staff dedicated to fraud, such as counter-fraud specialists or fraud examiners.

Whichever model an organisation uses, what is important is for the person responsible to be a 'counter-fraud professional'. 'Professional' has many connotations in both mainstream and academic debate. Central – and linked to a 'professional' – is the idea of a profession. Avoiding some of the extensive academic debates on what constitutes a profession, the central traits are:

- standards and a code of ethics;
- a body of knowledge disseminated by professional journals, conferences, etc.;
- a recognised association covering all aspects of the industry;
- institutions capable of training and evaluating personnel and awarding certification of competence;
- an educational discipline that is able to prepare students in the specific functions and philosophies.[1]

Elements of these exist to varying degrees in different countries. For example, in the USA there is the Association of Certified Fraud Examiners (ACFE) which has a standard of ethics, a knowledge base with dissemination structures (but no academic journal), a recognised training programme (Certified Fraud Examiner or CFE) and some degree level programmes at universities. ACFE also has a presence in the UK, but there is, in addition in the Institute of Counter Fraud Specialists (ICFS), recognised certification through the Accredited Counter Fraud Specialist award (ACFS) and degree programmes. However, even amongst those who have achieved ACFS, surveys of them in the UK have revealed substantial gaps in a professional infrastructure:

- Only around a quarter educated to at least graduate level.[2]
- Only around 13 per cent go on to achieve one of the higher awards of the CFPAB, such as CCFS.[3]
- Low levels of additional accredited training are undertaken.[4]
- Around three quarters are not a member of any professional association.[5]

There are further weaknesses in professional infrastructures which will now be explored. The next section will also set out a route map to the creation of a professional infrastructure, drawing upon the transformation of personnel management to Human Resource Management (HRM) in the UK.

10.2.1 Developing a Professional Infrastructure

A professional infrastructure also needs to be created that stimulates a culture of continuous improvement. Some of the weaknesses which currently exist include a lack of the following: a coherent body of knowledge, recognised professional representation, adequate training, education with proper entrance requirements and an enforced code of governance and ethics. It is clear from these weaknesses what needs to be done, and McGee,[6] drawing upon the work of Larson,[7] illustrates how the 'professional project' of personnel managers led to the emergence of a profession reborn under HRM. This model was achieved without any direct statutory intervention, which is another model to achieving a profession – through regulation.

A number of strategies were pursued by personnel managers to try to achieve the status of a profession.[8] McGee contrasts personnel managers in the 1970s and early 1980s to the situation today. He paints the picture of personnel managers with few if any specialist qualifications, neglected in strategic decision-making in the organisations they served, criticised by major government reports, such as the Donavon Commission, as lacking professionalism and represented by more than one professional association, with many not represented at all. This contrasts with a situation today where HRM has become a dominant model and personnel functions are integrated into the broader strategic goals of the organisation, although it would also be a fair criticism to say that many changes from personnel to HRM have been little more than name changes.[9] The two main representative associations, the Institute of Personnel Management and the Institute of Training and Development, merged in 1994 to create the Institute of Personnel and Development, which has since achieved the prestigious 'Chartered' status in the UK (which for most designates a true profession). Almost all of those working in HRM/personnel are members of this organisation, which boasts over 130,000 members. The Chartered Institute of Personnel and Development (CIPD) has a staff of 260, lobbies for the profession, is represented on many key forums, produces various publications, offers seminars and conferences, and provides a local branch structure.

Most significantly the CIPD has established a membership framework that begins with Affiliate, and moves through Associate, Licentiate and Graduate, rising to the Chartered grades of Chartered Member, Chartered Fellow and, finally, Chartered Companion. These grades carry weight, with many jobs advertised specifying a particular level, or that an expectation, such as a grade, will be achieved. Depending upon the level, the membership grades can be achieved through training, higher education and assessment of professional competence routes. The CIPD also has a code of ethics that, if breached, can lead to expulsion, something which in many positions means an end to working in HRM/personnel. The CIPD also does much to manage the image of the profession, to ensure it is portrayed in an appropriate light.

It is not just personnel managers in the field of management support functions who have managed to turn their occupation into a profession. Health and Safety managers are also much more advanced, with their Institution of Occupational Safety and Health (IOSH) having 32,000 members worldwide and 12,500 Chartered Safety and Health practitioners. Membership to this level is based upon the completion of a recognised course, usually a degree, masters or Level 4 course, combined with two years' experience and regular continuous professional development. IOSH also achieved chartered status in 2005. Another occupation with close links to counter-fraud is internal auditors. In the UK the professional association representing these received a Royal Charter in 2010 to become the Chartered Institute of Internal Auditors. It has a programme of advanced qualifications at graduate level linked to different levels of membership.

The above offers a 'route map' to a profession for those working in counter-fraud. The first and easiest step is for there to be one dominant professional association in a country. In the UK the picture is very fragmented, with a number of bodies which could emerge into this role, with ICFS in the strongest position. In the USA ACFE is in the prime place to achieve this position.

The dominant association then needs to create a suite of memberships which are linked to higher study and/or the equivalent. ACFE has the entry level CFE, but no higher awards. In the UK, the Counter Fraud Professional Accreditation Board, which is not a professional association, but does accredit and recognise training, has a learning route linked to higher education. The route is set out in Table 10.1 below.

Table 10.1 CFPAB Progression of Awards

CFPAB Award	Level
Accredited Counter-Fraud Technician	Various training providers provide and must be accredited by a higher education establishment to the equivalent of one twelfth of a first year of a Bachelor's degree.
Accredited Counter-Fraud Specialist, Accredited Counter-Fraud Manager, Accredited Counter-Fraud Intelligence Specialist	Various training providers provide and must be accredited by a higher education establishment to the equivalent of a third of a first year of a Bachelor's degree.
Certified Counter-Fraud Specialist	Completion of first year of recognised Bachelor's degree.
Graduate Counter-Fraud Specialist	Completion of recognised Bachelor's or Masters degree.

Any professional infrastructure should build upon the experience of the CFPAB and other professional bodies and have a structure such as the following:

- Entry Award – equivalent to first year of Bachelor's degree.
- Established Award – achieved after at least three years study/experience – equivalent to Bachelor's degree.
- Higher Award – based upon higher study or outstanding contribution to profession – equivalent to Master's level study.

In the UK context many professional associations link the above to categories of membership such as Student, Graduate, Member, Fellow, etc. Such categories encourage increased professionalism because ultimately most people want to progress up the ladder to enhance their own status and financial rewards.

It is not enough, however, just to create such a framework. The next step is to market and enforce it. All counter-fraud professionals should be encouraged to join, and those in positions of power recruiting new counter-fraud staff should specify the appropriate level of membership as an essential requirement.

The counter-fraud bodies should also learn from other representative associations and offer a range of services that further enhance professionalism. Assessing different bodies, some of the functions that should be provided are listed below:

- Annual conference
- Seminars on appropriate subjects
- Training
- Branch structure for knowledge transfer/networking
- Accreditation of training and academic courses
- Professional magazine
- Professional journal
- Conduct, commission and disseminate research
- Develop online resources
- Develop best practice and guides to specific security functions
- Sell publications at discount
- Publicise job opportunities
- Provide email alerts on latest information.

Many of these already exist, and deals could be pursued to provide them to members. For example, the *Journal of Financial Crime*, which is the closest the fraud world has to a professional academic journal, could be supplied as part of membership (many medical professional associations supply academic journals as part of their fees). A clear priority will be the need for an annual conference of counter-fraud professionals, which provides opportunities to share knowledge on the latest developments in countering fraud. Again, there are already many conferences that do this, but it is important for all to attend.

There is another area where such an association could have a very important role to play in enhancing the fight against fraud and that is to create structures where counter-fraud professionals can safely discuss their experience – including their failures. Learning from experience (or isomorphic learning) is central to enhancing the fight against fraud. Counter-fraud staff should be able to openly discuss fraud, 'behind the wire', amongst their peers under so-called 'Chatham House Rules' (what is discussed is not discussed outside the room). The development of such networks will greatly enhance isomorphic learning and overall, the improvement of the fight against fraud.

It is important to link such developments to codes of ethics and enforce the 'Chatham House Rules' in the code of conduct. This, however, is just one aspect of what the code should cover. Other aspects should include: to exercise functions with honesty and integrity; to adhere to appropriate laws and regulations; to abide by the rules of the association; to make a commitment to develop professionally; to respect the rights of minority groups and the importance of human rights, to name only some. The association should set such a code, publicise it to members and actively enforce it.

Most established professions have Centres of Excellence in some form which conduct research, identify best practice and have established networks for disseminating the best practice. The counter-fraud world is lacking in this. The Centre for Counter Fraud Studies is one of the few dedicated centres in academia focused upon fraud. It also hosts the Fraud and Corruption Hub which is a resource with links to the most significant research and publications on fraud. More of these need to be created around the world.

10.3 THE ESSENCE OF THE COUNTER-FRAUD PROFESSIONAL

This chapter has set out much of the professional infrastructure required. Ultimately, professionalism boils down to the operative who is employed to deal with fraud. This section will examine some of the traits which are required in a counter-fraud professional. As has previously been mentioned, the focus of counter-fraud staff is often on reactive investigations. There needs to be more than this, and the holistic approach as set out throughout this book means focusing upon proactive measures too. Therefore, the counter-fraud professional should focus upon:

- Monitoring fraud metrics and tailoring the strategy accordingly
- Preventative measures
- Developing an anti-fraud culture
- Detecting fraud as quickly as possible
- Investigating fraud
- Pursuing sanctions against those who have been caught which embrace all potential options: criminal, civil, regulatory and disciplinary
- Pursuing redress where possible.

In some organisations, the size of a counter-fraud department is such that there may be staff focused upon some of these. Nevertheless, it is important for the counter-fraud professional to have a grounding in all of these areas. The above is the broad set of knowledge required. There are other important traits which are also required and will now be examined.

10.3.1 The Enlightened Professional

Central to a counter-fraud professional is the need to be appropriately trained, educated and informed in the latest research and thinking relating to fraud. This can involve undertaking short training courses or enrolling upon a counter-fraud related degree or master's programme. It can also mean attending conferences and seminars as well as reading professional magazines and journals. It is also important that these are pursued on a regular basis – what is more commonly known as continuing professional development (CPD). Underpinning this is the need – where there is evidence – to pursue evidence-based solutions to the problems the organisation faces. The box below lists some of the key sources of knowledge and training/education.

Information on Latest Research

The Fraud and Corruption Hub – http://www.port.ac.uk/ccfs
Wiley – http://eu.wiley.com/WileyCDA/
Gower – http://www.ashgate.com/
Journal of Financial Crime – http://www.emeraldinsight.com/products/journals/journals.htm?id=jfc

Fraud News

ACFE Fraud Magazine – http://www.fraud-magazine.com/
Fraud Intelligence – http://www.informaprofessional.com/publications/newsletter/fraud_intelligence
Fraudwatch – http://www.fraudwatchonline.com/

Fraud Courses

ACFE – http://www.acfe.com/
Centre for Counter Fraud Studies – http://www.port.ac.uk/ccfs
Fraud degrees and higher training courses – http://www.larry-adams.com/university_fraud_courses.htm
PKF – http://www.pkf.co.uk/pkf/services/forensic/counter_fraud_services/home

Professional Associations

ACFE – http://www.acfe.com/
ICFS – http://www.icfs.org.uk/

10.3.2 The 'Reflective' Professional

Based upon the original ideas of Schon,[10] who advocated 'reflective practice', where professionals are expected to reflect regularly on their work and learning, there is much use for the counter-fraud professional. Schon argues that professionals face two sets of problems at the high and low ground. On the high ground, it is argued that problems are well defined as are the strategies to deal with them, frequently based upon extensive research. Take, for example, the principles of building a bridge – there are many factors to bear in mind with guidance based upon much research. On the 'swampy lowlands', however, there are also many problems which are messy, with no simple solutions and it is here where the most significant threats are, according to Schon. To use the bridge analogy again, however, when the type or decision whether to build a bridge is considered, the technological knowledge is lost in the political, financial, environmental and various other factors that confuse what decision to make. Reflective practice (and the related action research) can help solve these problems. This approach has gained much favour amongst some healthcare professions. Nurses, clinical educators, physiotherapists, occupational therapists and radiographers, as well as managers, are some of the occupations that have been encouraged to combine the theory aspects of their course with reflection on their professional practice.[11] By its very nature it is difficult to set out an approach to pursue reflective practice, but Palfrey sets out the following:

- The need to reflect critically on what one does as a counter-fraud professional and on what happens as a result of one's practice.
- A regular re-examination of one's experience, beliefs and conceptual knowledge.
- The generation of new perspectives and knowledge arising from reflections on action (reflecting after one's actions) and reflection in action (reflecting during one's actions).
- The welcoming of challenges to one's standard way of thinking about and acting on problems.[12]

Given the unique challenges faced by counter-fraud professionals, which are often in the 'swampy lowlands', the 'reflective practice' model would seem well suited to the counter-fraud professional. Nevertheless, in an organisation dominated by practice based upon evidence from research, the difficulty of applying reflective approaches does pose problems.

10.3.3 The Counter-Fraud Leader

Not all counter-fraud professionals will need to be leaders, but many will. Leadership is to be distinguished from management. Sperry[13] argues that, typically, management is distinguished by the functioning of individuals under conditions of stability focused upon tasks such as meeting objectives, assessing compliance and coordinating staff and work patterns. By contrast, leadership is aligned on more unstable conditions and times of change, and focuses upon inspiring and/or galvanising the commitment of staff. However, he goes on to argue that this distinction does not reflect the research and that 'effective management and leadership cannot be separated'. The contrasting aspects of management and leadership are required for success and the theme of his book is that they are complementary. Underpinning this debate is the basic problem of there having been much research on leadership, but little agreement on what leadership and management are.[14] Nevertheless, the distinction above, if accepted, does raise scenarios where the two sets of skills conflict. As Villiers and Adlam[15] argue:

> The cautious, artful, consensus-seeking manager – who knows the cost of everything and upsets no-one, and whose quota is always fulfilled – may be quite incapable of swift and dynamic leadership when the situation requires it.

Before we begin to discuss what makes an effective manager/leader, it would be useful to clarify some of the terms used in such debates.

- **Skills**: how to's of a function which are transferable from person to person
- **Knowledge**: what a person knows
- **Talents**: natural abilities in a person
- **Competencies**: expected behaviours.

If we use an analogy faced by some counter-fraud professionals, such as dealing with a potentially violent situation with a fraudster who has just been identified, knowledge would be the ability to recognise certain non-verbal behaviours in a person and skills would be applying the appropriate strategies to the person to calm them down. There may, however, be certain people that have a natural talent to be able to cope with an aggressive person because of their character. The competency is to be able to calm an aggressive person without using force, which for some might be based upon skills and knowledge learnt, while in others, talent.

However, when competencies are examined they often reveal conflicts. A skill may be identified, which is actually a talent. For example, being able to make effective decisions in a pressure situation might be a talent, rather than a skill that can be learnt. And if competencies are based on talents, the expected behaviour might be very difficult to achieve. Sperry[16] argues that competencies should be purely skills-based and the most effective leaders are those who can identify the people with the appropriate talents and who then develop the missing skills and knowledge in them. These leadership and management skills are the most important determinant of an organisation's success, '... more important than industry, environment, competition and economic factors combined' according to Whetten and Cameron.[17] Sperry[18] goes on to outline 12 essential skills that underpin the effective leader and these are set out below:

Operational

1. Galvanising commitment and motivation
2. Maximising team performance
3. Delegating to maximise team performance
4. Managing stress and time effectively.

Relational

1. Communicating effectively and strategically
2. Negotiating and managing conflict and difficult people
3. Coaching for maximum performance and development
4. Counselling and interviews for maximum performance and development.

Analytic

1. Thinking and deciding strategically
2. Mastering the budget process
3. Mastering and monitoring financial and human resources
4. Assessing corporate and personal resources.
5. Adapted from Sperry.[19]

10.4 REDEFINING THE COUNTER-FRAUD PROFESSIONAL

A theme running throughout this book is how fraud can bring competitive advantage. This is central to the redefinition of the counter-fraud professional. They must speak the language of business, such that what they advocate will produce a reward to the organisation in reduced fraud losses, which mean either increased profitability or, in the public sector context, reduced taxation or more resources to spend on essential services. The counter-fraud professional needs to redefine the perception that countering fraud is an additional cost on the bottom line, to a benefit to the bottom line. The following are central to achieving this:

10.4.1 Pursuing the Holistic Model of Countering Fraud Advocated in This Book

This book has set out the key elements of an approach to counter fraud that brings competitive advantage. These centre around accurate measurement of fraud losses, a strategy tailored to the risks, appropriate investment in prevention and the development of an anti-fraud culture, quick detection of fraud, professional investigation of fraud, the pursuit of the full range of sanctions and redress and the development of appropriate metrics.

10.4.2 Redefining the Lexicon of Countering Fraud

The counter-fraud professional also needs to use the appropriate lexicon of the modern business world and deliverers of public services. This is increasingly pre-occupied with reducing costs, increasing efficiency, improving profitability, etc. The counter-fraud professional needs to know what fraud, and the response to it, is costing the organisation and what can be done to reduce it. Knowledge of metrics, return-on-investment, financial costing models are all central. It is also important to be attuned to the objectives of the organisation and how countering fraud can enhance them. The contrast between the old and new lexicons is set out below:

Old: limited knowledge of impact of fraud (detected at best), a service for the organisation that is a cost, a focus upon detection and investigation.

New: accurate knowledge of costs of fraud, financial benefit to the organisation, integrated, holistic approach, a focus on prevention.

10.4.3 Communicating the Rewards to the Wider Organisation, and Particularly the Leaders, of Successfully Countering Fraud

It is also important for the counter-fraud professional to evangelise the benefits of the modern approach across the organisation. This, as well as adding to the effort to create an anti-fraud culture, makes clear the positive impact countering fraud is having on the organisation. Not to do so risks questions arising over the benefit of spending large sums of money on countering fraud. This invariably makes counter-fraud resources more vulnerable when the organisation faces financial difficulties, as it is often seen as an easy area to cut. Therefore, communicating the work of counter-fraud professionals to all levels of the organisation is very important.

10.4.4 Securing Positions of Influence Within the Organisation

Linked to effective communication is the importance of securing positions in the most influential committees, forums, etc. of an organisation, and, if this is not possible, forging direct links to those who are. In the related field of security management, there has been much written on the lack of influence in the boardroom.[20] This is also the case for many counter-fraud professionals. In most organisations a place on the board is unlikely for a counter-fraud professional, but a direct report to someone who is on the board is achievable. The board itself should periodically be exposed to reports on fraud and the progress in dealing with it. Other influential forums within the organisation should also be targeted to ensure there is a counter-fraud presence. This ensures that decisions are not made which might unintentionally increase the level of fraud.

10.5 THE COUNTER-FRAUD DEPARTMENT

Discussions surrounding the counter-fraud professional inevitably lead to whether there should be a counter-fraud department and what shape that should be. The authors believe that the more important issue is the quality and orientation of the staff the organisation has access to – the counter-fraud professional(s). The structures that they operate within the organisation depend a great deal upon the organisational context. In some organisations, such as insurers, a counter-fraud department might be appropriate; in a university, one or more staff in the audit department with other functions too might be appropriate. Having high quality staff with the appropriate mentality is the most important factor in making the most of whatever organisational structure exists.

Another important element related to the structures is the various regulations concerning corporate governance. Companies from the USA, or operating there, are subject to the provisions of the 2002 Sarbanes-Oxley Act and in the UK there has been the Turnbull Corporate Governance code, amongst others. It is not the aim of this book to become embroiled in the intricacies of the requirements and the utility of these requirements. Where they are the law, it is the duty of an organisation to comply. However, the model set out in this book is the most important consideration in reducing fraud. What is clear with the corporate governance agenda is that major frauds and corruption still occur even when organisations are in compliance.[21]

10.6 CONCLUSION

This chapter has explored the person of central importance in an organisation in countering fraud: the counter-fraud professional. It began by examining who the counter-fraud professionals are, before highlighting some of the weaknesses in a professional approach. The broader professional infrastructure was then examined and this showed a number of weaknesses. The experience of the transition of personnel management to HRM was then demonstrated and offered as a route map for counter-fraud professionals. A number of potential reforms to achieve this were examined. The chapter then ended with a consideration of the counter-fraud professional at an individual level and some of traits and orientations that are required for them to become professionals.

FURTHER READING

Bryman, A. (1986) *Leadership and Organizations*. London: Routledge and Kegan Paul.

Button, M. (2008) *Doing Security: Critical Reflections and an Agenda for Change*. Basingstoke: Palgrave

Monks, R.A.G. and Minow, N. (2010) *Corporate Governance*. Chichester: Wiley.

Schon, D. (1983) *The Reflective Practitioner: How Professionals Think in Action*. New York: Basic Books.

END NOTES

1. Larson, M.S. (1977) *The Rise of Professionalism: A Sociological Analysis*. Berkeley: University of California Press; Manunta, G. (1996) The Case Against: Security Management is Not a Profession. *International Journal of Risk, Security and Crime Prevention*, 1: 233–240; Simonsen, C.E. (1996) The Case For: Security Management is a Profession. *International Journal of Risk, Security and Crime Prevention*, 1: 229–232.
2. Button, M., Johnston, L., Frimpong, K. and Smith, G. (2007) New Directions in Policing Fraud: the Emergence of the Counter Fraud Specialist in the United Kingdom. *International Journal of the Sociology of the Law*, 35: 192–208.
3. Ibid.
4. Ibid.
5. Ibid.
6. McGee, A. (2006) *Corporate Security's Professional Project: An Examination of the Modern Condition of Corporate Security Management, And the Potential for Further Professionalisation of the Occupation*. MSc Thesis, Cranfield University.
7. Larson, op cit.
8. Button, M. (2008) *Doing Security: Critical Reflections and an Agenda for Change*. Basingstoke: Palgrave.
9. Armstrong, M. (2006) *A Handbook of Human Resource Management Practice*. London: Kogan Page.
10. Schon, D. (1983) *The Reflective Practitioner: How Professionals Think in Action*. New York: Basic Books.
11. Palfrey, C., Thomas, P. and Phillips, C. (2004) *Effective Healthcare Management*. Oxford: Blackwell.
12. Ibid, p. 37.
13. Sperry, L. (2003) *Becoming An Effective Healthcare Manager*. Baltimore: Health Professions Press.
14. Bryman, A. (1986) *Leadership and Organizations*. London: Routledge and Kegan Paul.
15. Villiers, P. and Adlam, R. (2003) *Introduction*. In Adlam, R. and Villiers, P. (eds) *Police Leadership in the Twenty-first Century*. Winchester: Waterside, p. xii.
16. Sperry, op. cit.
17. Whetten, D. and Cameron, K. (2002) *Developing Management Skills*. Upper Saddle River, NJ: Prentice Hall, p. 5.
18. Sperry, op. cit.
19. Ibid, pp. 7–8.
20. See Challinger, D. (2006) Corporate Security: A Cost or Contributor to the Bottom Line. In Gill, M. (ed) (2006) *The Handbook of Security*. Basingstoke: Palgrave; Garcia, M.L. (2006) Risk Management. In Gill, M. (ed) *The Handbook of Security*. Basingstoke: Palgrave; Gill, M., Burns-Howell, T., Keats, G. and Taylor, E.

(2007) *Demonstrating the Value of Security.* Leicester: Perpetuity Research and Consultancy International; Gill, M., Taylor, E., Bourne, T. and Keats, G. (2008) *Organisational Perspectives on the Value of Security*. Leicester: Perpetuity Research and Consultancy International.

21. Monks, R.A.G. and Minow, N. (2010) *Corporate Governance*. Chichester: John Wiley & Sons.

11

Reaping the New Competitive Advantage

11.1 INTRODUCTION

In this final chapter we return to the central theme of the book and bring together the arguments made throughout. In an era of tighter budgets and more competitive markets, organisations are looking for innovative ways to reduce costs. Many strategies and innovative ideas have been pursued, from contracting out to flatter management structures, to achieve what is often described as 'competitive advantage'.[1] One measure which has not been on the 'radar' of the vast majority of organisations to achieve this aim is investing in measures to counter fraud. This book has shown how fraud is a major cost, how it can be measured, but most significantly how a comprehensive approach can be created, which has been proven to substantially reduce this cost. This final chapter will bring together the key aspects of this strategy and then show how average returns could impact on the profitability of the world's leading companies.

11.2 BRINGING THE COUNTER-FRAUD STRATEGY TOGETHER

Throughout this book we have set out a case for fraud to be treated like any other business cost and a model to reduce that cost, which is proven, and which can bring substantial benefits for the organisation in reaping a competitive advantage.

Figure 11.1 was originally produced for the UK Government as part of its 'Fraud Review' project to make the UK the hardest target for fraudsters of any country in the world.[2] It brings together the arguments made in this book – sequentially – showing what an organisation needs to do to have the most effective strategy. As can be seen, the new approach involves:

- Obtaining a high level of knowledge about the nature and extent of the 'fraud problem' ideally through fraud loss measurement;

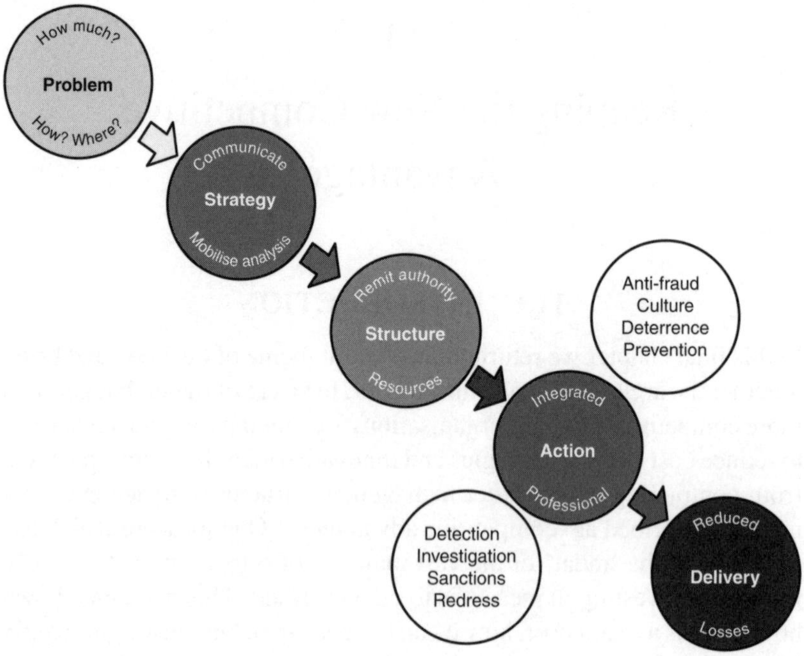

Figure 11.1 The Professional Approach to Countering Fraud

- Designing and communicating a strategic solution to the 'problem', which reflects the specific knowledge obtained about it;
- Creating a structure which has the remit, authority, skills and resources to implement the strategic solution;
- Using the structure to take a range of proactive and reactive action; and
- Delivering measured, tangible outcomes in respect of reduced losses.

Central to this is also having professionally trained staff to undertake these functions and to detect and investigate fraud as well as seeking the appropriate sanctions and redress according to the circumstances of the case. Developing an anti-fraud culture and fraud prevention are also very important functions. This integrated action, it is argued, culminates in reduced losses and therefore increased profitability or resources to spend on services. The following section will demonstrate what these benefits could be to an organisation.

11.3 REAPING THE BENEFITS

Fraud can lead to less financially stable and healthy companies and its reduction can also significantly improve profitability; it can result in public services which are not of the quality that citizens pay their taxes to get, and its reduction can allow the maintenance and improvement of those services; it can result in the goods and services which we purchase as consumers being more expensive than they should be, and its reduction can significantly improve value for money; charities can see their charitable purposes undermined by fraud, and its reduction can allow additional resources to be focused on important deserving causes. These positive outcomes arise from the financial benefits derived from the reduction of the significant cost which fraud represents.

This chapter provides an unprecedented insight into the benefits to private companies of reducing the cost of fraud. In uncertain macroeconomic times, cutting the cost of fraud – revealed by the latest global research to represent, on average, 5.7 per cent of expenditure – can massively boost profitability and financial health. Developments over the last decade or so, to accurately measure the cost of fraud like any other business cost, has allowed organisations from many different sectors, and across the world, to manage and minimise that cost.

If you don't understand the nature and scale of the problem how can you apply the right solution? Over the last decade or so it has become possible to accurately measure the nature and scale of fraud – and then to design an informed strategy to address it. Fraud is a challenging problem. Its economic effects are clear. In every sector of every country, fraud has a pernicious impact. However, historically, fraud has been described as 'difficult to cost' and until relatively recently, it has not been possible to quantify these effects. In the last 10–15 years this situation has changed and as Chapters 2 and 5 revealed, it is possible to accurately measure fraud costs.

The Financial Cost of Fraud Report 2011[3] represents the latest, most extensive global research in this area. The report documents what has been found across the world, over the period from 1997 to 2009. It also shows the impact of the recession on losses by comparing and contrasting data from 2008 and 2009 with the prior period. It focuses on presenting a credible, accurate and statistically valid picture, in a context where the quality of some information has historically been poor.

There are still some estimates published which are simply not reliable. Counting only those losses which are detected or prosecuted, or surveying those working in the area for their opinion, will never be accepted as reliable indicators of the real economic cost of fraud.

Unless one imagines that all fraud can be detected – and research tends to indicate that, at best, organisations can only detect in the region of 1/30th of it – then a measure of fraud based on detected losses will always represent a serious underestimate.[4] Bearing in mind that even the crime of murder doesn't have a 100 per cent detection rate and that the essence of fraud is about concealment, it is unlikely ever to be the case that what is detected will represent the totality of the cost.

Surveys of opinion are also unreliable. The Association of Certified Fraud Examiners (ACFE) in the United States produces an annual survey of this type.[5] Its most recent edition states that 'survey participants estimated that the typical organisation loses 5 per cent of its annual revenue to fraud'. Such surveys can represent a reliable reflection of the opinion of those surveyed (if the sample is representative) but, in the absence of an examination of actual items of expenditure, and the collation of evidence of correctness, error and fraud, they are not grounded in fact.

It is now possible to do much better than this. The financial cost of fraud and error can be accurately measured in the same way as other business costs. This is not unnecessarily costly or difficult and, most importantly, an accurate, statistically valid figure can be provided for what the financial cost is estimated to be.

Let's remind ourselves again of what the cost of fraud is to society. The latest global research indicates that losses average 5.7 per cent of expenditure. When measured across 32 types of expenditure with a total value of £5 trillion, and in several different countries, just under 70 per cent of accurate and statistically valid measurement exercises revealed losses of 3 per cent or more. This figure rose to over 75 per cent for the period after the recession of 2008–2009 (see Figure 11.2).[6]

So, research leaves little room for doubt that fraud represents a significant cost.

The global average loss rate of 6.1 per cent for the period after the recession commenced (2008–2009), when taken as a proportion of the global Gross Domestic Product (GDP) for 2010 ($62.91 trillion or £40.66 trillion),[7] equates to £2.48 trillion, a sum equivalent to more than one and a half times the UK's entire GDP. Applying this loss rate to UK GDP (£1.45 trillion for 2010) equates to losses of more than £88 billion.[8]

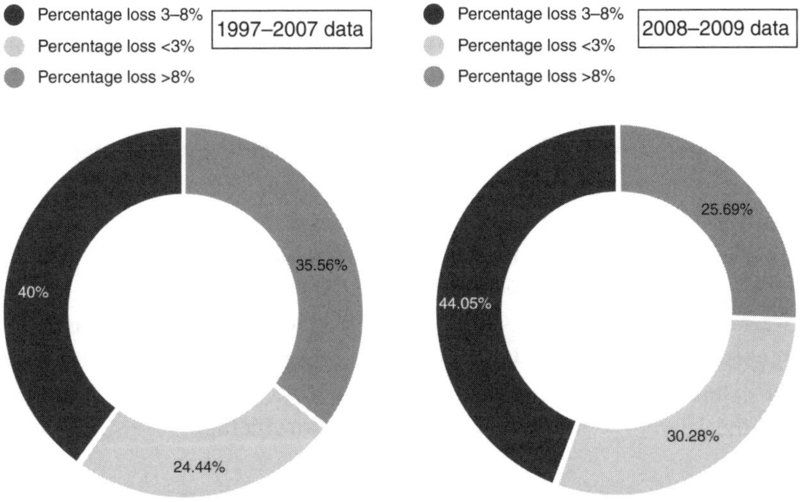

Figure 11.2 Comparing Fraud Losses by Amount

In the global healthcare sector, the average percentage of expenditure lost across such a wide range of healthcare expenditure, was found to be 7.29 per cent.[9] The World Health Organisation's latest estimate of global healthcare expenditure is US $5.7 trillion. Thus, it is likely that around US $415 billion is lost globally to fraud (and error). This is the equivalent of more than twice the budget for the entire UK NHS or enough to build more than 2,300 new hospitals (at developed world prices) and more than the entire national GDP of all but 29 of more than 190 countries across the world. Countering fraud effectively would reduce these losses and free up massive resources for better patient care.

In the UK, the Government's National Fraud Authority (NFA), in its Annual Fraud Indicator for 2012, estimates that £73 billion is lost to fraud, with £20.1 billion lost in the public sector.[10]

So, it is clear that the cost of fraud is significant and can be and has been measured in many different types of organisation. The next logical question concerns the extent of the competitive advantage to be gained from reducing this cost and how quickly it can be realised.

11.4 HOW QUICKLY CAN LOSSES BE REDUCED AND BY HOW MUCH?

Organisations have been measuring and reducing other types of business cost for decades – usually with progressively smaller reductions as time has gone by – but they have mostly not been doing this in respect of the cost of fraud. Indeed, it is still possible to hear those leading sizeable private or public sector organisations comment that 'there is no fraud in my organisation'. Such comments show a lack of understanding that the first step to solving a problem is to stop being in denial about it. Even where such attitudes are not prevalent, it is still common for organisations to have a reactive approach, acting primarily after fraud has taken place and after the losses have been incurred.

The Financial Cost of Fraud Report 2011 refers to examples where losses have been reduced. Where losses have been measured, and the organisations concerned have accurate information about their nature and extent, they have been substantially reduced. The best examples over the 12 year period covered by this Report include:

- the UK's National Health Service (the second largest organisation in the world) between 1999 and 2006 where losses were reduced by up to 60 per cent, and by up to 40 per cent within 12 months;[11]
- the US Department for Education, which reduced its losses across a $12 billion dollar grant program by 35 per cent between 2001 and 2005;[12]
- the US Department of Agriculture, which reduced its losses across a $12 billion dollar programme by 28 per cent between 2002 and 2004;[13] and
- the UK's Department of Work and Pensions which has successfully reduced its losses in Income Support and Job Seekers Allowance by 50 per cent between 1997/98 and 2005/06.[14]

These are published public sector examples because of the transparency requirements concerning public expenditure. However, there are unpublished private sector examples, which the authors of this report are aware of, showing a comparable position. In fact, research shows that the position concerning losses does not vary significantly according to what part of the economy an organisation comes from.

Even during the two years after the start of the recession, and in the middle of a period during which fraud losses increased by over 30 per cent,[15] two of the organisations included in this research reported very significant reductions in their losses – one by 33 per cent and the other by 19 per cent – within a single year in each case. As can be seen, the speed of reduction of losses will vary from organisation to organisation, but it is not unreasonable to assert that losses can be reduced by

40 per cent over a two year period – this is what the data shows. What would such a reduction in losses mean?

This section of the chapter reviews data from across the world to provide an answer. An assumption has been made, in the absence of company-specific data on losses, that the companies reviewed suffered the average loss revealed by the most comprehensive research in this area. Projected financial benefits from reducing those losses have been based on a 40 per cent reduction, in accordance with evidence where such reductions have been achieved.

11.5 THE WORLD'S 500 LARGEST COMPANIES

In the global commercial sector, fraud has a significant effect on profitability. The Fortune 500 ranking of the world's 500 largest companies for 2011 shows that they had total annual revenues exceeding $26 trillion, with profits of over $450 billion, representing 1.75 per cent of revenues. Applying the global average loss rate (5.7 per cent), derived from where losses have been accurately measured, would imply that losses total $1.48 trillion, more than three times the total profits of these top companies.

What would such a reduction in the cost of fraud mean in financial terms? The beneficial effects in the commercial sector are startling. 326 of the world's largest companies would increase their profitability by between 10 and 99 per cent; 124 would do so by between 100 and 1000 per cent; 24 would be making profits not losses and 11 would have reduced losses. This would represent a massive boost to corporate health and would point the way out of one of the worst global recessions ever.

The average increase in profitability (excluding one outlier), across the 463 firms who were already profitable to some extent, would be almost 124 per cent. Among the 11 firms which were making losses (of $68.2 billion), those losses would be reduced by an average of over 26 per cent ($17.8 billion) (see Figure 11.3).

The proportion of companies that would increase their profitability is indicated below: 90 per cent would increase their profitability by 10 per cent or much more. Almost 25 per cent would more than double their profitability, with some increasing their profitability by up to 1000 per cent (see Figure 11.4). And of course, the beneficial effects do not stop there. Greater profitability can enable greater investment, more competitiveness, an increase in employment, increased tax revenues and a general economic stimulus.

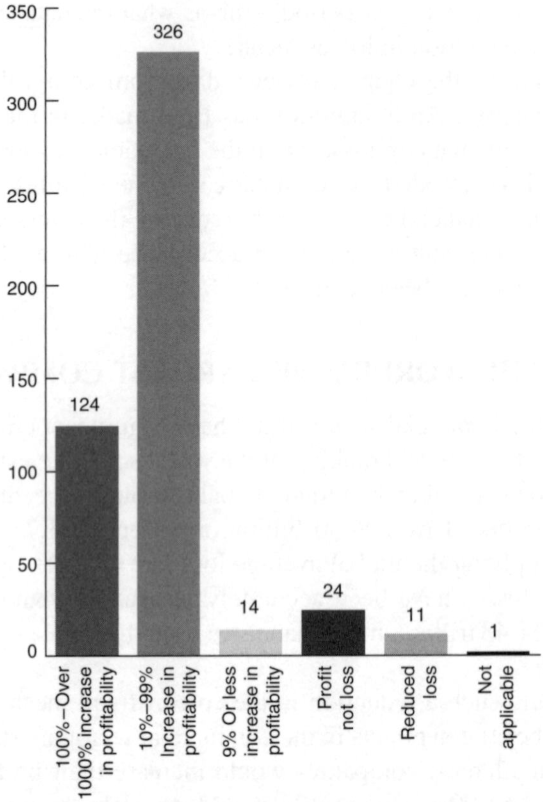

Figure 11.3 Fortune 500 Increases in Profitability by Number

11.6 UK FTSE 350 COMPANIES

Data from the latest financial results were reviewed concerning 272 FTSE 350 listed companies. Full datasets relating to some companies were not available. They had total annual revenues of more than £1.52 trillion, with net pre-tax profits of almost £173 billion, representing 11.3 per cent of revenues. Applying the global average loss rate (5.7 per cent), derived from where losses have been accurately measured, would imply that losses total almost £87 billion, more than half as much again.

What would such a reduction in the cost of fraud mean in financial terms? The beneficial effects in the commercial sector are clear. Fifty-three of the FTSE 350 companies would increase their profits by up to 9 per cent; 190 would increase their profitability by between 10 and

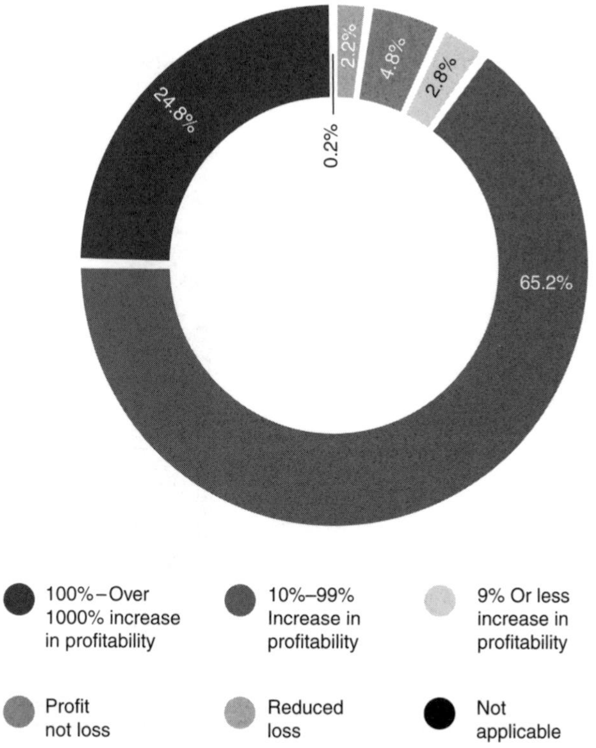

Figure 11.4 Fortune 500 Increases in Profitability by Percentage

99 per cent; 11 would do so by between 100 and 1000 per cent; one would do so by over 1200 per cent; 4 would be making profits not losses and 13 would have reduced losses (see Figure 11.5).

The average increase in profitability (excluding one outlier), across the 255 firms who were already profitable to some extent, would be almost 36 per cent. Among the 13 firms which were making losses (of £610 million), those losses would be reduced by an average of over 57 per cent (over £350 million).

The proportion of companies that would increase their profitability is as follows: 70 per cent would increase their profitability by between 10 and 99 per cent or much more. 4.4 per cent would more than double their profitability, with one increasing their profitability by over 1200 per cent (see Figure 11.6). As the UK Government struggles to grow the economy's way out of the recession, this could be a significant factor.

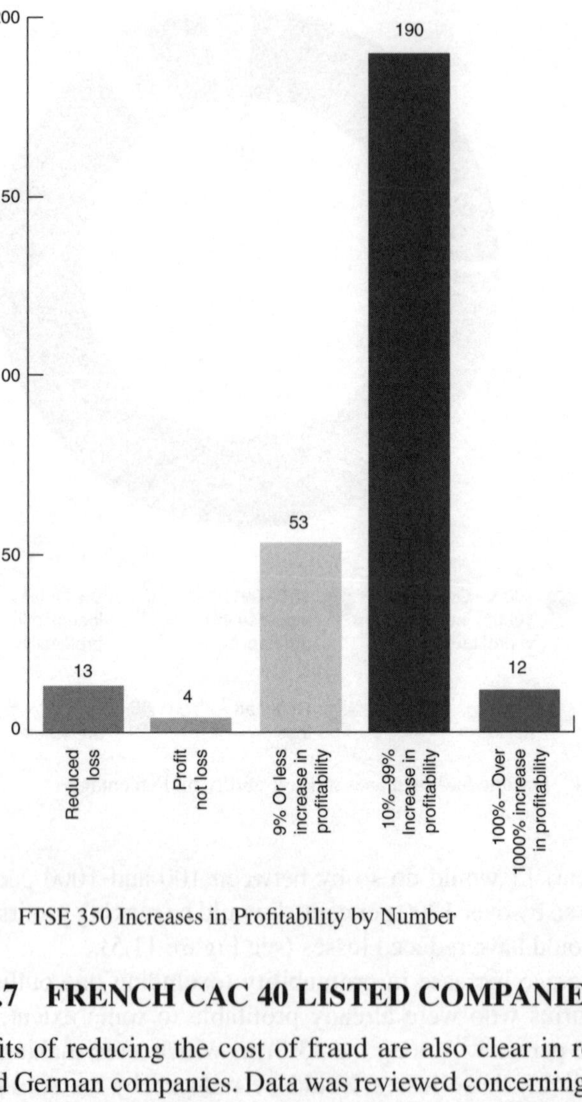

Figure 11.5 FTSE 350 Increases in Profitability by Number

11.7 FRENCH CAC 40 LISTED COMPANIES

The benefits of reducing the cost of fraud are also clear in respect of French and German companies. Data was reviewed concerning 26 CAC listed companies. Full datasets relating to some companies were not available. They had total annual revenues of more than €865 billion, with net pre-tax profits of almost €278 billion, representing over 32 per cent of revenues. Applying the global average loss rate (5.7 per cent), derived from where losses have been accurately measured, would imply that losses total over €49 billion. What would such a reduction in the cost of fraud mean in financial terms? All of the 26 companies would increase their profits – and by a range of between 2.5 and 25 per cent. The average increase in profitability would be 7.8 per cent.

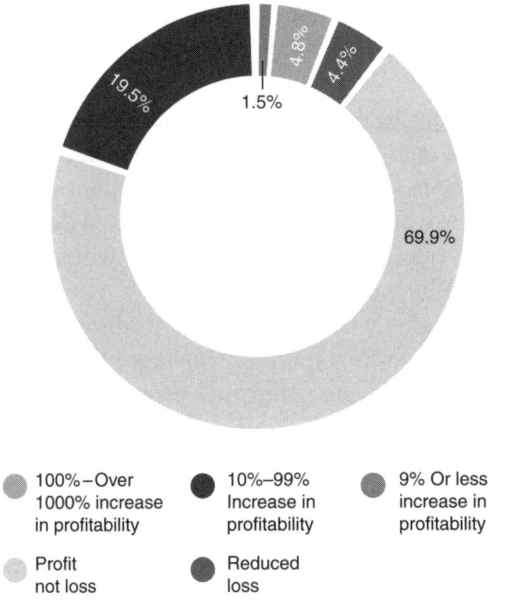

Figure 11.6 FTSE 350 Increases in Profitability by Percentage

11.8 GERMAN DAX 100 LISTED COMPANIES

Data was reviewed concerning 69 DAX listed companies. Full datasets relating to some companies were not available. They had total annual revenues of more than €1.04 trillion, with net pre-tax profits of almost €283 billion, representing over 27 per cent of revenues. Applying the global average loss rate (5.7 per cent), derived from where losses have been accurately measured, would imply that losses total over €58 billion. What would such a reduction in the cost of fraud mean in financial terms? All of the companies would increase their profits – and by a range of between 2 and 125 per cent. The average increase in profitability would be 10.1 per cent.

11.9 CONCLUDING REMARKS: REAP THE ADVANTAGE!

No matter whether companies are listed in the UK, USA, France or Germany (or other countries around the world, as in the case of some Fortune 500 companies), cutting the cost of fraud can significantly boost profitability. The competitive advantage to be derived from the measurement and reduction of the cost of fraud could not be clearer. By ensuring that resources are not diverted from where they are intended to be applied, there are real competitive and financial advantages to be reaped.

We now have the tools to accurately measure fraud as a business cost, and to focus our skills and resources on reducing that cost. Rapid reductions have been shown to be possible and there are very significant financial benefits which can be delivered. As with any new way of doing things, the question initially was 'Why would we do that?' It is now becoming 'Why wouldn't we do that?'

This book highlights why and how organisations can start to manage their fraud costs, just as they routinely manage other costs. The statistics revealed indicate that private companies probably have the most to gain from this approach. In a difficult macro-economic climate, the benefits of cutting the cost of fraud could provide a real economic stimulus.

As with other significant developments in business, the new approach is simply a result of looking at a problem in a different way, and then developing the related methodologies. The barriers to progress are often in the mind rather than in reality. If you consider fraud just to be a crime, then you police it; if you think of it as a business cost like any other then you manage and reduce it. The new approach has now been tested in organisations from across the world and has delivered proven results. And, as ever, now that this has happened, those who follow next will reap the greatest competitive advantage.

FURTHER READING

To secure access to the largest resource base for counter-fraud articles and research reports you should register with the Centre for Counter Fraud Studies to access the Fraud Hub. This can be done at: http://www.port.ac.uk/departments/academic/icjs/centreforcounterfraudstudies/fraudhub/.

END NOTES

1. Porter, M.E. (2004) *Competitive Advantage*. New York: Free Press; and Briggs, R. and Edwards, C. (2006) *The Business of Resilience*. London: Demos.
2. Fraud Review Team (2006) *Final Report*. Retrieved 28 July 2006 from http://www.aasdni.gov.uk/pubs/FCI/fraudreview_finalreport.pdf.
3. Gee, J., Button, M. and Brooks, G. (2011) *The Financial Cost of Fraud. What the data from around the world shows*. London: PKF/CCFS.
4. NHSCFSMS (2007) *Countering Fraud in the NHS: Protecting Resources for Patients. 1999–2006 Performance Statistics*. London: CFSMS.

5. ACFE (2010) *Report to the Nation on Occupational Fraud and Abuse*. Austin: ACFE.
6. Gee et al., op. cit.
7. IMF Data – Nominal GDP list of countries for the year 2010. World Economic Outlook Database – September 2011.
8. Ibid.
9. Gee, J., Button, M. and Brooks, G. (2011) *The Financial Cost of Healthcare Fraud. What the data from around the world shows*. London: PKF/CCFS.
10. National Fraud Authority (2012) *Annual Fraud Indicator*. London: NFA.
11. NHSCFSMS (2007) op. cit.
12. United States Department of Education (2001) Fiscal Year 2001 Accountability Report. Retrieved 20 April 2010 from http://www2.ed.gov/about/offices/list/ocfo/FY2001AccountabilityRpt.pdf; United States Department of Education (2005) FY 2005 Performance and Accountability Report. Retrieved 20 April 2010 from http://www2.ed.gov/about/reports/annual/2005report/edlite-index.html.
13. United States Department of Agriculture (2002) Performance and Accountability Report FY 2002. Retrieved 20 April 2010 from http://www.ocfo.usda.gov/usdarpt/par2002/pdf/par2002.pdf; United States Department of Agriculture (2003) Annual Report for Fiscal Year 2003 Report on Performance and Accountability. Retrieved 20 April 2010 from http://www.ocfo.usda.gov/usdarpt/par2003/pdf/par2003.pdf; United States Department of Agriculture (2004) 2004 Performance and Accountability Report. Retrieved 20 April 2010 from http://www.ocfo.usda.gov/usdarpt/par2004/pdf/par2004.pdf .
14. Department for Work and Pensions (2007) *Fraud and Error in the Benefits System April 2005 to March 2006*. London: Department for Work and Pensions.
15. Gee et al., op. cit.

Index

Index compiled by Terry Halliday